W9-CDE-606

SOTHEBY'S ART AT AUCTION 1997–1998

SOTHEBY'S

ART AT AUCTION 1997–1998

First published in 1998 by
Sotheby's
34–35 New Bond Street
London W1A 2AA

Copyright © Sotheby's 1998

Sotheby's is a registered
trademark.

All rights reserved. No part of
this book may be reproduced,
stored in a retrieval system, or
transmitted in any form or by
any means, electronic,
electrostatic, magnetic tape,
mechanical, photocopying,
recording, or otherwise
without the prior permission of
the publisher.

British Library Cataloguing in
Publication Data

A catalogue record for this
book is available from the
British Library.

ISBN 0–9622588–9–x

Project Editor: Emma Lawson
Associate Editor: Renée du Pont
Harrison
Assistant Editor: Malcolm
Cossons
Production Controller: Chris
Smith
Art Editors: Sally Jeffery and
Suzan Aral, Jeffery Design
Art Director: Ruth Blacksell

Printed in Germany by
Mohndruck, Gütersloh

ENDPAPERS: A view of
HRH The Duke of Windsor's
bedroom. The Collection of
HRH The Duke and the
Duchess of Windsor
(see pages 34–35)

HALF TITLE: Claude Monet,
*Bassin aux nympheas et sentier
au bord de l'eau*, signed and
dated 1900, oil on canvas,
89 by 100 cm (35 by 39⅜ in),
London £19,801,500
($33,068,505) 30.VI.98
(see pages 24–25)

FRONTISPIECE: *La Chasse aux
Faucons* (detail), a late Gothic
falconing tapestry, Tournai, *c.*
1520, 350 by 320 cm (11 ft 6 in
by 10 ft 6 in), London £749,500
($1,259,160) 3.XII.97. This
result represents a new world
auction record for a tapestry.

TITLE PAGE: Alexandra
Vasilievna Shchekotikhina-
Pototskaya, *Motherhood Plate*,
diameter 26.7 cm (10½ in),
London £17,250 ($28,290)
19.11.98. From the Nicholas
Lynn Collection of Soviet
Revolutionary Porcelain
(see page 10)

THIS PAGE: Chang Yu (Sanyu),
Goldfish, signed SANYU in
English and *yu* in Chinese in a
square, oil on canvas, 73.5 by
50 cm (29 by 19⅝ in), Taipei
NT$7,200,000 (£131,195;
$218,911) 19.X.97 (see page 16)

PAGE 192: Billy Stockman
Tjapaltjarri, *Wild Potato (Yala)
Dreaming*, 1971, synthetic
polymer powder paint on
composition board, 54.5 by
46 cm (21½ by 18⅛ in),
Melbourne A$200,500
(£72,180; $118,295) 29.VI.98

CONTENTS

INTRODUCTION

Diana D. Brooks

As this year's *Art at Auction* amply demonstrates, the 1997–98 auction season at Sotheby's was both memorable and historic. Fine art and antique buyers the world over stepped forward to compete vigorously at the highest levels, resulting in numerous world record prices being achieved for individual artists, as well as for rare or unusual works of art. The success of the auction year was, without question, highlighted by a number of impressive single-owner sales, most notably that of the collection of HRH The Duke and the Duchess of Windsor. An enormous undertaking by any standard, this landmark sale captured the attention of over 30,000 bidders from 50 different countries.

On the pages that follow, we have featured a diverse selection of intriguing objects, fine art and special sales that demonstrate the impressive results achieved during the autumn 1997 and spring and summer 1998 sales. As you will see, Impressionist and Contemporary Art, Old Master Paintings, Asian and American Art, and English and Continental Furniture all achieved outstanding results. From the unprecedented offering of a dinosaur named 'Sue' to the sales in London and New York of two of Claude Monet's finest paintings, the results recorded within are a testimony to a thriving, competitive auction environment. Fittingly, we have dedicated the cover of *Art at Auction* to Andy Warhol's incomparable *Orange Marilyn*, a quintessential icon of Pop Art that achieved a price almost four times the previous world record for the artist.

The momentum that distinguished the past 12 months at Sotheby's came in combination with two important events. In January 1998, we celebrated the opening of our new premises in Paris, France at the famed Galerie Charpentier. In August, we began construction for the expansion of our salesrooms in New York City. These two expansion projects will enable us to serve our clients in the years ahead, years which no doubt will be distinguished by an increasingly competitive art market.

We hope that this comprehensive review will encourage one and all to join us at auction in the upcoming months where together we can witness exciting auction results such as those featured on the following pages.

Diana D. Brooks
President and Chief
Executive Officer, Sotheby's

OPPOSITE *Baigneuse* by Pierre-Auguste Renoir, signed and dated *88*, was sold at Sotheby's New York on 13th November 1997 for $20,902,500 (£12,332,475), setting a new world auction record for the artist.

SOTHEBY'S YEAR IN EUROPE

Henry Wyndham

Henry Wyndham is Chairman of Sotheby's Europe.

RIGHT This life-size Safavid portrait of a European dignitary, c. 1660–90, was sold in October 1997 for £441,500 ($715,230). Previously unrecorded, it is one of only 12 such paintings known to exist.

A review of the 1997–98 auction season provides a welcome opportunity to look back and assess the general state of the market, discern recognizable trends, acknowledge the unexpected and, in turn, look forward to the next season.

All signs indicate that the art market is buoyant, with new price levels being achieved across a range of disciplines, in many cases exceeding those reached in the heady days of 1990. Figures published in the Art 100 Index, an analysis of art sales in the West, show that prices went up by 30.6% in the 12 months to the end of July 1998, and auction results from Sotheby's European salesrooms bear this out. Such results are encouraging, not least because they point to a solid, healthy market made up of discerning collectors. Gone are the speculators of the late 1980s whose tastes seemed indiscriminate and whose mass buying artificially inflated results.

A spectacular example of the current state of the market was the sale of Claude Monet's *Bassin aux nympheas et sentier au bord de l'eau* (see pages 1, 24–25) in London on 30th June. Not seen on the market for almost 50 years, the appearance of this seminal work at auction was a last-chance opportunity for the interested buyer. Five telephone bidders initiated the bidding, with two taking it to a final £19,801,500 ($33,068,505), which was greeted by applause. This price was the highest in London for a decade, the third highest ever achieved at auction in the city, the 11th highest in the world and a new auction record for the artist. It is proof, if such is needed, that London is the centre of a strong art market and has much to offer the discriminating buyer.

Further evidence of the strength of the market in Europe, and just two of the many examples available, are the record-breaking sales of Old Master paintings (discussed by Alexander Bell on pages 18–19) and Contemporary art. The total for London's sale of the latter in July was £11.9 million ($19.7 million), the highest since 1990, and a post-sale analysis showed that eight of the top ten lots were bought by Europeans.

Sotheby's has recently made a considerable investment in two key locations in Europe and the Middle East: Paris, France and Tel Aviv, Israel. The company has had an office in Paris since 1967 and held its first sale in Monaco in 1975. Now, in anticipation of forthcoming legislation, it has moved its headquarters in France to the elegant Galerie Charpentier, Paris's premier auction house from the late 1930s to 1950s. Here legendary masterpieces and collections were sold and important exhibitions mounted, with visitors including artists, world leaders and royalty. Now restored to its original 19th-century glory, it is again equipped to stage major sales and exhibitions.

The Galerie Charpentier opened to the public in March with an inaugural exhibition devoted to masterpieces of furniture from French private collections, many of which had not been seen in public before. Of particular note was the *Teschen* table loaned

by the Marquis de Breteuil, which is made of semi-precious stones mounted in gilt-bronze and silver-gilt.

Sotheby's Israel had much to celebrate in 1998 with the 50th anniversary of the founding of the State of Israel and the auction house relocation to new premises in Tel Aviv's booming financial district. A number of exciting additions were made to the auction schedule, including the innovative inaugural sale of Young Art. This offered the work of art students and recent graduates at estimates that ranged from $200 to $3,000. Young and eager buyers attracted by the works' quality and affordable prices ensured that this auction was 100% sold. We plan to repeat the sale in 1999.

The London salesrooms were also witness to a number of successful innovations and the continued strength of established sales. Islamic Week, in place for almost three decades, has now been joined by Asia Week, which was launched in New York in 1992. This series of sales provides collectors with access to related areas within an international setting. Despite the fluctuations of the Asian economy, all categories performed well, an auction record was set for a Chinese Export dinner service (see page 124) and several Chinese works of art significantly exceeded their estimates. The sale of Contemporary Indian paintings demonstrated the consolidation of this market, with

artists such as Chughtai (see page 11) developing a strong auction presence.

The expediency of uniting related works in one event was seen in the 9th June sale of Important British Pictures, which spanned more than four centuries. Among its highlights were Sir Joshua Reynolds's portrait of Lady Williams Wynn and her three children (see page 11), John Frederick Herring Senior's *Shoeing Imaum* (see page 57) and the *Rhinebeck* panorama. The four watercolour panels of the panorama measure 9 feet in length and form a detailed record of the streets, buildings and everyday life in London at the time of the Napoleonic wars. The painting takes its name from Rhinebeck, New York where it was discovered lining a gun barrel in 1940. Sold for £199,500 ($325,185), its buyer was revealed to be the Museum of London, where it will go on display once conservation work is complete.

A further welcome addition to the London auction calendar was the Political Sale, held on 15th July. Rich with items associated with Britain's main political parties and their members, this event generated considerable interest from Parliament, public and press, exceeding its pre-sale estimate to achieve a total of £821,768 ($1.3 million). In particular demand were pieces that had belonged to Sir Winston Churchill, including his top hat (right), cigar case and slippers,

ABOVE Jack B. Yeats's painting *Singing 'Oh, Had I the Wings of a Swallow'* set a new auction record for the artist when it achieved a price of £881,500 ($1,428,030) in Sotheby's fourth Irish Sale.

BELOW Sir Winston Churchill's black plush top hat was sold in London's Political Sale for £25,300 ($41,239).

evidence of the continued popularity of this great statesman. Another aspect of Churchill's life was on display in January when Sotheby's mounted a major exhibition of his paintings in the Bond Street galleries, 50 years after his election by the Royal Academy as an Honorary Academician Extraordinary. An insight into the importance to Churchill of this 'pastime' was given by his daughter, Lady Soames, in the accompanying catalogue: 'I am convinced that this compelling occupation played a real part in enabling him to confront storms, ride out depressions and to rise above the rough passages of his political life.'

The success of events like the Political Sale highlight the extent to which we are all connected to our past and wish to conserve, and own, the evidence that remains. Every season at Sotheby's brings reminders of world history, and 1997–98 was no exception. Even a small selection of the items can give a sense of the centuries spanned, countries of origin and categories encompassed by the auction house's sales. For example, in December 1997 Sotheby's London offered the Edith Hahn Archive for sale (see page 112). This group of letters, documents and photographs revealed the incredible and often devastating events that surrounded Hahn's survival as an Austrian Jew in the Second World War. Two American businessmen bought the archive for almost five times its estimate and have donated it to the US Holocaust Memorial Museum in Washington.

The enormous propaganda effort that followed the Russian Revolution was on display in January when the Nicholas Lynn Collection of Porcelain was offered for sale (see page 3). Large amounts of undecorated material, found in the Imperial Porcelain Factory, were painted by the Bolshevik designers with striking images and, in many cases, stern directives, such as the plate in the collection that read: 'He Who Does Not Work Does Not Eat'.

May and June brought to auction two groups of photographs that stand as a unique record of a particular time and place. The first under the hammer were daguerreotypes dating from the 1850s to the 1890s, which had been commissioned by the 8th and

TOP The head office of Sotheby's France is now based in the famed Galerie Charpentier, Paris.

ABOVE Sotheby's new landmark residence in Tel Aviv has been restored to its former glory – an elegant Tuscan-like villa of the early 20th century on the tree-lined Rothschild Boulevard.

9th Earls of Elgin, documenting the countries in which they served, particularly Canada and India (see page 101). In June a set of the earliest extant photographs of Mecca and Medina, taken by Sadiq Bey in 1880–81, achieved a new auction record when they sold for £1,376,500 ($2,257,460, see page 113).

Three pieces of furniture intimately connected with royal history were sold in July. The Warwick tables, originally owned by Queen Anne and more recently displayed at Hampton Court (see page 29), were joined in the English Furniture sale by the Marot table. Unrecognized for over 300 years, including a period in which it was used by Cecil B. DeMille as a film prop, this piece was rediscovered by Adriana Turpin of Sotheby's Institute when she ascertained that its label reading 'La Galerie Thames' referred to the Water Gallery at Hampton Court Palace during the reign of William and Mary. It sold for £331,500 (£540,345). Also in this month Sotheby's was able to announce the sale by private treaty of the Sherborne Missal to the British Library (see pages 40–41). Described as 'one of Britain's greatest national treasures', this 536-page, 40-pound illuminated manuscript is the only late medieval monastic service book of such stature to have survived the Reformation intact.

Works of art can also enter the annals of history through their provenance. This season Sotheby's has been privileged to offer items that have belonged to the famous collectors of the past, such as William Beckford (see page 137), Henri Vever (see page 129) and Prince Marcantonio IV Borghese (see page 28), and the great collectors of the present, including Lord and Lady Sainsbury (see page 84), José Luis and Beatriz Plaza (see page 86) and Hashem Khosrovani (see page 121).

This is only the briefest selection of highlights from Sotheby's year in Europe. In the following pages readers will find a range of objects from our many salesrooms that have achieved memorable results. This review leads one on to anticipate the as yet unknown highlights of the forthcoming season and I hope that I will have the opportunity of welcoming you to our galleries where, perhaps, you may see history being made.

In June Sotheby's held a special sale of Important British Pictures. Just one of its many highlights was the *Portrait of Lady Williams Wynn with her Children* by Sir Joshua Reynolds, which sold for £1,376,500 ($2,243,695). The painting is now hanging in the National Gallery of Wales.

RIGHT An 18th-century Dutch Hebrew prayer book containing daily prayers for the year was sold in Tel Aviv for $156,500 (£93,900) in the spring of 1998.

FAR RIGHT *Krishna and Radha* by the artist Abdur Rahman Chughtai was sold for £34,500 ($56,580) in the sale of Contemporary South Asian and Indian art, just one of the events that made up Sotheby's successful Asia Week in London.

The Arrival of Prince Humbert, the Rajah, at the Palace of Amber was executed in 1888, at the height of Edwin Weeks's Indian oeuvre. Offered in the May sale of Nineteenth Century European Paintings, its price ($1,157,500; £694,500) was almost twice the pre-sale high estimate.

Richard E. Oldenburg is Chairman of Sotheby's North America.

With high points encompassing Warhol and Windsor, Rembrandt and Renoir, 1997–98 was a gratifying auction year for Sotheby's in North America. Record prices were achieved in many areas of the fine and decorative arts, as well as in more obscure categories such as scrimshaw and mechanical robots. However arcane, works of extraordinary quality or rarity attracted discerning collectors and generous bids.

Sales of Impressionist and Modern works achieved excellent results in the autumn and spring series. The November sales, which included the Evelyn Sharp Collection and paintings by Paul Cézanne formerly in the collection of Auguste Pellerin, totalled $155.9 million (£92 million), the highest since the autumn of 1990. Among 31 paintings selling for more than $1 million were two exceptional works by Renoir:

Baigneuse (see page 6) and *La coiffure* ($8.8 million; £5.2 million). Notable works from the Sharp Collection included Picasso's exuberant *Nus* from 1934 (see page 89), and his classic period *La toilette de Venus* (1923), which brought $4.95 million (£2.9 million). From the ten paintings by Cézanne once owned by Auguste Pellerin, the most avid collector of the artist's works, there were the early painting, *Une moderne Olympia* (see page 80), and a large example from Cézanne's bather series, *Cinq baigneuses* ($5.5 million; £3.2 million).

The Impressionist and Modern sales in May brought a total of $108 million (£66 million). In this field, where demand increasingly exceeds supply, strong prices were achieved at both the high and the mid-market levels. The top lot, *Le Grand Canal* by Monet, an entrancing memento of the artist's first visit to Venice,

achieved substantially more than its sale price of $9.9 million at the market's peak in 1990 (see page 25). Other highlights were *Après le bain* by Degas (see page 81) and *La cheminée* by Bonnard (see page 87). Also featured were nine paintings from the Collection of Rolf and Margit Weinberg, which set auction records for Gustave Courbet, Theo Van Doesburg and Oscar Schlemmer. The Part II Impressionist and Modern sale reached $30 million (£18 million), the highest total since the spring of 1990.

This was also a notable year for sales of Contemporary Art, with both the autumn and spring series producing totals not seen since 1990. At $38 million (£23 million), the November sale exceeded its high estimate and set auction record prices for eight artists. Among these were Bruce Nauman (see page 92) and Mark Rothko,

whose *No. 14, 1960* (see page 91) was purchased by the San Francisco Museum of Modern Art.

The Contemporary sale in May was a memorable event, with many attendees attracted by the extraordinary works on offer, including the quintessential icon of Pop Art, *Orange Marilyn* by Andy Warhol (see cover and page 26). In an otherwise hushed salesroom, a progressive bidding contest produced a final price almost four times the previous Warhol record at auction. Another outstanding work was Lucian Freud's *Large Interior w11 (after Watteau)*, recognized as a masterpiece of 20th-century British painting (see page 27). Auction records were also set for Carl André, Jean-Michel Basquiat, Damien Hirst and Mike Kelley.

This was a banner auction year in other areas of the fine arts. The December sale of American paintings

Included in the record-breaking sale of Old Master paintings at Sotheby's New York in January, this *View of the Isola della Giudecca with the Church of Il Redentore, Venice* by Francesco Guardi achieved $1,322,500 (£806,725).

The Ortiz-Patiño Collection of Books and Manuscripts, offered in April 1998, included the 15th-century Hours of Saint-Lô, represented here by an illumination showing the Annunciation to the Shepherds. It set a new auction record for a French book of Hours when it achieved $3,632,500 (£2,179,500).

achieved $43.7 million (£25.8 million), setting a new record in this category, surpassing that set at Sotheby's in 1989. The top lot was one of six paintings in the sale by John Singer Sargent, the enchanting *In the Garden, Corfu* (see page 72). Several artist records were also set, including those for Georgia O'Keeffe (see page 74) and Stuart Davis (see page 75). The May sale was highlighted by 44 works from the outstanding Eulich Collection of Western Art, which achieved a record total for a single-owner American paintings sale (see pages 22–23).

The field of Old Master paintings also enjoyed remarkable success this year. The January sale in New York, at $53.2 million (£32 million), set a new world auction record in this category – the third time in a row for Sotheby's Old Master sales in New York and London – and established 12 artist records. The highlight was

Rembrandt's recently discovered *Portrait of a Bearded Man* (see page 44), which achieved the second highest price for the artist at auction. In the preceding sale of Old Master Drawings, the extremely rare opportunity to acquire a large-scale drawing by Michelangelo produced a new record for a drawing by this artist (see pages 20–21).

The success of the sales of Nineteenth Century European Paintings reaffirmed Sotheby's leading position in this field. In October, Winterhalter's *Jeune fille de l'Ariccia* achieved $1.8 million (see page 62) contributing to a solid total of $12.9 million (£7.9 million). The subsequent two-day series of sales in May realized $22.5 million (£13.5 million), the highest total ever achieved by an auction in this category. In a buoyant salesroom, active bidding produced 15 artist records. Among the highlights were nine paintings by Bouguerreau and *Le salon du peintre*, a masterwork by Alfred Stevens which is also known as the *Vanderbilt Stevens* after the family that owned it for almost a century (see page 66).

Latin American works of art fared well this year. The November sale marked the 20th anniversary of Sotheby's New York auctions in this field and yielded an impressive total of $12.4 million (£7.3 million). Featured were 12 paintings from the Barratt-Brown Collection, including Diego Rivera's rich Cubist painting, *Nature morte avec géranium* (see page 77). In May Wifredo Lam's *La mañana verde* achieved a price second only to the record set by the artist's *Ogue Orisa*, sold by Sotheby's in November (see page 79). Eleven new auction records were also set for artists from Brazil, Venezuela, Uruguay and Ecuador.

In the burgeoning field of photography, new highs were achieved this year. The April sale included Edward Weston's 1924 *Circus Tent*, a rare image from his Mexican years (see page 102), and Man Ray's *Champs délicieux*, a book of rayographs published in 1922, which brought $244,500 (£146,700). These were the two most expensive lots sold in any auction of photographs during the 1997–98 season.

For Asian art, this season was the most successful to date. The March 1998 series of Asia Week sales set a world record, with a total of more than $17 million (see pages 38–39). The Indian and Southeast Asian art sale was highlighted by a Gupta red sandstone head of Buddha from the estate of Earl Morse, which achieved the highest price ever paid for an Indian sculpture at auction (see page 122).

This was also a strong year for the decorative arts. In

the week-long January series of Americana sales, more than 2,400 lots were offered, including items from the collections of Stanley Paul Sax (see pages 32–33), and the Masco Corporation. The sales produced a total of $25.8 million (£15.7 million), the highest in auction history, with record prices achieved in several categories.

The November sale of Highly Important French Furniture, including property from the Collection of Mrs Antenor Patiño and the Estate of Mrs Charles Allen, was notably successful, with a total of $11.7 million (£6.9 million). This was also a memorable year for French silver with the sale of the Thyssen Meissonnier Tureen in May (see pages 30–31). The October sale of Magnificent Jewellery was also one of the strongest offerings in recent years, bringing a total of $37 million (£22 million), and the spring sale in May achieved an additional $17.1 million (£10.3 million).

In the autumn of 1997, two special sales attracted particular interest and attention. In October Sotheby's had the privilege of offering one of the world's most celebrated dinosaur fossils, the largest and most complete skeleton of a *Tyrannosaurus rex* ever found. Nicknamed 'Sue' after its discoverer, it was sold to the Field Museum of Natural History in Chicago, where it will be seen by generations of visitors in years to come (see page 42).

In December Sotheby's auctioned the property of the legendary composer and conductor, Leonard Bernstein. The crowds that attended the exhibition and sale, as well as the total achieved of $1.1 million (£0.7 million), evidenced the admiration and respect with which Bernstein is recalled.

However, the most extraordinary event, for which this season will long be remembered, was the sale of the collection of HRH The Duke and the Duchess of Windsor (see pages 34–35). Originally planned for September 1997, this long-awaited sale was postponed following the deaths of Diana, Princess of Wales and Mr Dodi Fayed, son of the collection's consignor. Rescheduled to February 1998, this became the longest sale in American auction history, with the collection's 44,000 objects achieving a total of $23.4 million (£14.3 million), more than three times the pre-sale high estimate. Public and press interest was intense, attesting to the enduring fascination of the Windsors' historic romance. The sale's great success was also the product of imaginative foresight and meticulous care in planning and execution and, as such, was an impressive and well-earned tribute to the dedication of Sotheby's staff members.

This Louis XVI mahogany *fauteuil en cabriolet* still bears the label of its painter and gilder, Louis Chatard, which indicates that it was destined for the use of Queen Marie Antoinette, whose initials appear on the top rail. It sold on 25th April 1998 for $475,500 (£285,300).

Property from the Estate of Leonard Bernstein was offered for sale in December, a portion of the proceeds from which benefited the Bernstein Education Through the Arts (BETA) Fund. His Bösendorfer semi-concert grand piano, inscribed by Bernstein with his signature and a heart, sold for $387,500 (£236,375).

Alice Lam

Alice Lam is Co-Chairman of Sotheby's Asia.

For Sotheby's in Asia October 1997 was notable for two things: the beginning of the sales season, and the beginning of the Asian economic crisis. It was going to be an extremely challenging time.

Although Asian currencies were fluctuating, the September sale of Southeast Asian paintings in Singapore was relatively unscathed. The Taiwan-based auctions followed and suffered no significant effect from the financial downturn; indeed, Robert Frank's collection of paintings by Sanyu (see page 4) achieved the kudos of being a 'white glove' sale when all 21 paintings sold. Credit for this must go to Rita Wong, then Chairman of Sotheby's Taiwan, who not only masterminded the sale but also contributed substantially to establishing Sanyu's name in the art market. After almost 20 years' service at Sotheby's, Rita has decided to retire from the auction field but remains a non-executive member of Sotheby's Asia Management Board.

This rare 'Clair-de-Lune' dish from the Yongzheng period was part of a European private collection of Chinese ceramics sold in Hong Kong on 5th November. It achieved HK$1,450,000 (£112,403; $187,339).

The base of a Ming blue and white dragon brushwasher, which established a new world auction record for Ming blue and white porcelain when it sold on 5th November 1997 in Hong Kong for HK$16,520,000 (£1,280,620; $2,134,367).

Belgian artist Adrien Jean Le Mayeur de Merprès settled in Bali in 1932 and his resulting work reflected life on the island. This example, *Two Women Shaded by an Umbrella*, c. 1935, achieved a world record for the artist when it sold for S$608,750 (£224,630; $375,772).

The November sales in Hong Kong were anticipated with optimism due to the inclusion of a fine collection of ceramics, sculptures and falangcai, a prestigious private collection of paintings by Zhang Daqian, dazzling jewels and our inaugural watch sale. Our clients did not stay away; they stayed and bought. An auction record for Ming blue and white porcelain was set when a dragon brushwasher (opposite, below) fetched HK$16,520,000 against an estimate of HK$9–10 million. The Camélias de Jade, a jadeite brooch and earclips ensemble designed by Chanel (right), attracted worldwide attention long before the sale began; it sold to an overseas telephone bidder for HK$4,970,000 (£385,271; $642,119). The first watch sale made an immediate impact, with more than 90% sold and a world auction record achieved for a Patek Philippe.

By spring 1998 the economic storm was raging. Sotheby's Taipei faced it first, yet the Chinese oil paintings sale brought satisfactory results. Hong Kong was next and, against the odds, weathered the storm by taking the lead and holding the first wine auction on the island: 90% of the lots were sold and the auction realized HK$6.4 million (£0.5 million; $0.8 million, see page 179). The second watch sale followed the success of the first by almost doubling the previous total. Chinese art and jewellery sales were smaller and buyers were cautious. However, a jadeite necklace realized HK$9.9 million (£0.8 million; $1.3 million, see page 164), becoming the highest selling jewellery item in all of Hong Kong's spring auctions. The stamp market too, with the support of our private collectors, maintained an even keel.

The season closed with remarkable results from Singapore's Southeast Asian Paintings sale. Held at

Designed by Chanel Joaillerie to reflect Coco Chanel's interest in symbols, colour and texture, the Camélias de Jade achieved HK$4.9 million when it was offered at Sotheby's Hong Kong in November.

another financial crisis point, this event earned international recognition when a world auction record was achieved for the artist Adrien Jean Le Mayeur de Merprès (above, top).

Even with the volatility of the Asian economy over the past nine months, the results of Sotheby's sales have proved that there is still a desire in these countries to buy at auction. In addition, our Asian clients extended their buying to Sotheby's salesrooms worldwide, from Los Angeles to Zurich and house sales in England.

The autumn sales season will see auctions in a wide range of collecting areas and an exciting new venue for our Hong Kong sales at the Conrad International Hotel. With these sales and with our continued dedication to client service and expertise, Sotheby's looks forward to reaching new high ground in Asia.

A GOLDEN AGE: OLD MASTER PAINTINGS AT SOTHEBY'S

Alexander Bell

Alexander Bell is a Senior Director and Head of the Old Master Paintings department, Sotheby's London.

TOP Sotheby's January sale in New York included the dramatic *Eruption of Vesuvius* by the relatively unknown artist Pierre Jacques Antoine Volaire. It achieved $1,212,500 (£739,625), a price that a good Canaletto might have realized only a few years ago.

The 1997–98 season was a remarkable one for Old Master paintings, with Sotheby's sales in London in December 1997 and New York in January 1998 becoming the two most successful events of this type ever held. In the aftermath, one respected commentator concluded that Old Masters had 'entered a new art market golden age'. Certainly these results, which were the latest in a series of ever improving sales that had, to some extent, mirrored the increasing buoyancy of Western economies, and had seen an influx of new buyers in the field, would seem to bear out this analysis. But this is a broad and sophisticated market, representing over six centuries of artistic production in Western Europe, and many forces are at work in determining how a painting will be received.

Tastes for different artists and schools of painting change over time. This season underlined the fact that works by Dutch and Flemish 17th-century artists are now much sought-after. An unusually large supply at auction of masterpieces from sources rich in these schools, notably the collections of the British Rail Pension Fund and the Steinberg, Fattorini and Henle families, has helped to fuel the market. Prices have also risen as collectors in this area, who are predominantly based in North America and Northern Europe, have become richer as these economies have boomed. The main reason behind the success of this field, however, lies in the type of images such works usually depict: accessible and attractive subject matter, often on a modest scale, which fits particularly well into today's domestic environment

One striking feature of the market in general is how price differentials have increased: the phenomenon whereby two paintings by the same artist can realize hugely differing prices. Three principal factors are at play: condition, image and provenance, and all can be illustrated by examples from the 1997–98 auction season.

The state of preservation of a painting is an increasingly important factor in determining its price. Collectors want a work to look as close to the artist's original intention as possible. If a picture has suffered through damage – usually caused by clumsy or over-zealous restoration – its appeal, and value, will be far less. Pieter Brueghel the Younger's *Village Scene* (opposite, below) was in near perfect state, and it was this factor, as much as any other, that pushed its price to a new world record for the artist.

A painting with an attractive image, such as the portrait by Johannes Verspronck sold in January (see page 45), will naturally command a higher price than one with an unappealing subject. But the extent of this price difference has now reached greater levels than ever before.

The provenance of a painting has always influenced the price, but today it is the length of time that a picture has been away from the market, as much as its earlier history, that influences its reception. To possess both is ideal and such circumstances helped to raise the price of Isack von Ostade's *A Waggoner and Other Figures Halted at an Inn* (opposite, above) to a world record level.

As great paintings by major artists have become increasingly expensive, so we have seen another development: the rise in prices for exceptional works by artists outside the front rank (see above). Most collectors would rather pay more for an outstanding work by a lesser artist than for an average production of a first-rank painter.

As we approach the new millenium I believe the pattern that has emerged during the 1990s, outlined here, will continue, with certain areas of the market that have been overlooked, such as neo-classical painting and 18th-century Dutch landscapes, seeing greater levels of growth.

LEFT Isack van Ostade's depiction of figures outside an inn fetched £2,201,500 ($3,698,520) in December 1997. It was last seen on the market in 1959 when it entered the Henle Collection and had earlier belonged to the Prince de Talleyrand and the Baring family.

BELOW *Village Scene* by Pieter Brueghel the Younger was sold in London in December 1997 for £1,981,500 ($3,328,920), establishing a standard by which other pictures coming on to the market will now be judged.

CHRIST AND THE WOMAN OF SAMARIA BY MICHELANGELO

Gregory Rubinstein

Gregory Rubinstein is Worldwide Head of Old Master Drawings at Sotheby's.

In New York on 28th January 1998, Sotheby's sold one of the most important Renaissance drawings to have appeared on the market for many years: Michelangelo's magisterial, late double-figure study representing *Christ and the Woman of Samaria*. Only a handful of Michelangelo's known drawings remain in private hands and, of those, this is without doubt the most substantial, moving and significant. The sheer scale of the figures is larger than in any of his other drawings that is not a full-scale cartoon for a painting, and the rugged, sculptural power of the draughtsmanship, as well as the profound and reflective emotional intensity of the drawing, place it among the most beautiful and important drawings by this artist.

Although the exact dating of the drawing within Michelangelo's career has been much discussed (most recently and thoroughly by Dr Paul Joannides in an article in *Sotheby's Preview*, January 1998), it is clear that it is a late work, executed some time between the early 1540s and the late 1550s. By that time Michelangelo's work had taken on a deep religious spirituality, often, as here, expressed through serene and simple compositions that explore on a monumental scale the relationship between two figures within a Biblical context. In this case, Michelangelo's interpretation of the theme seems to have grown out of a project conceived in the early 1540s for a finished, composition drawing of the same subject, to be executed as a token of his admiration for poet and patron Vittoria Colonna, with whom Michelangelo had an intense, intellectual friendship during the latter years of his life. That presentation drawing has not survived, but it is known through a print by Nicolas Béatrizet (right), which shows it to have been a much more static and emotionally detached work than the surviving composition.

During the two and a half centuries following its creation, *Christ and the Woman of Samaria* passed through several important collections, most notably those of the early 17th-century Florentine, Cardinal Antonio Santa Croce, whose original mount is preserved with the drawing, and the celebrated early 18th-century French connoisseur, Pierre Crozat.

Following a sale in 1807, the drawing disappeared from view and, despite its importance, remained unpublished until 1981. By that time, it was in the collection of the Foundation established by the noted Swiss bibliophile Martin Bodmer, at Cologny, near Geneva, where it remained, seen only by a small number of specialists in the field. The Trustees of the Foundation eventually took the decision to sell the drawing in order to establish a permanent fund for acquisitions in the institution's core areas of activity, namely printed books and manuscripts. Understandably, the appearance on the market of such an important yet little-known work by one of the masters of the Italian Renaissance excited enormous interest, and highly competitive bidding between two private collectors drove the price to $7,482,500 (£4,564,325), a world auction record for a Michelangelo drawing, and the highest price ever achieved at Sotheby's for an Old Master drawing.

An engraving by Nicolas Béatrizet of *Christ and the Woman of Samaria*, after Michelangelo's lost presentation drawing for Vittoria Colonna.

The recto of Michelangelo Buonarroti's drawing *Christ and the Woman of Samaria*, with a separate sketch of *A Man Looking Up, His Arms Raised*. Inscribed MICHELANGELO, the drawing is in black chalk with traces of white chalk and measures a maximum height of 43.5 cm (17 in).

THE JOHN F. EULICH COLLECTION OF WESTERN ART

Peter Rathbone and
Dara Mitchell

Peter Rathbone and **Dara
Mitchell** are both Senior
Vice Presidents and Heads
of the American Paintings,
Drawings and Sculpture
department, Sotheby's
New York.

The December 1997 and May 1998 sales of American
paintings, drawings and sculpture demonstrated
the continued strength of the market. These events,
which achieved the two highest sale totals for American
paintings in auction history, reaffirmed Sotheby's
leadership in the field. In addition, the landmark sale of
The John F. Eulich Collection in May was one of the
highlights of the season, totalling $25 million (£15.5
million), $4 million over its pre-sale high estimate.

The Eulich Collection represented the most
comprehensive group of paintings depicting America's
western heritage assembled by a private collector in the
past 20 years. It included seminal works by artists such
as Frederic Remington, Albert Bierstadt, William T.
Ranney, George Catlin and John Mix Stanley, many of
whose paintings are rarely available on the auction
market. Mr Eulich, who began forming the collection in
1978, is a visionary collector who became well-known
for the dynamic quality of his acquisitions, which he
pursued based on each work's artistic excellence.
Between September 1991 and January 1995, the
collection was exhibited in 11 prominent American
museums and its appearance at auction was greeted
with tremendous enthusiasm. By the close of the sale,
26 new auction records were set for artists including
Seth Eastman, Joseph Henry Sharp, Henry F. Farny,
Charles Schreyvogel, Oscar Berninghaus, Walter Ufer
and E. Martin Hennings. This remarkable single-owner
sale eclipsed that of the landmark IBM Collection,
which achieved a total of $19 million in 1995.

The two top-selling lots were paintings by Frederic
Remington, America's most celebrated western artist,
who depicted the US cavalryman – undisputed hero of
the American West – in many of his most important
canvases. *The Trooper*, which sold to an anonymous
private collector for $2,532,500 (£1,570,150, see page
71), was painted between 1891 and 1902 and reflects the
artist's unabashed admiration for military life on the

RIGHT E. Martin Hennings moved to Taos, New Mexico in 1921 and found artistic inspiration in the people of the Pueblo and villages and their surroundings. In *Four Riders*, Hennings creates a harmonious composition through the careful placing of the Indians on horseback within a landscape.

OPPOSITE, ABOVE Executed in 1869, 14 years after John Mix Stanley's last trip to the West, *Blackfeet Card Players* captures the daily life of the Prairie Indian as recalled by the artist from his many years painting portraits of Indians in the western territories. Nearly all of the North American tribes gambled, card playing being one of the few pastimes the Native Americans garnered from white society.

OPPOSITE, BELOW By the time he painted *The Apaches!* in 1904 Frederic Remington's images of these characters from the West were based entirely on nostalgic memories of a disappearing past, a romanticized vision of the West Remington had imagined, experienced and loved but which no longer existed. In 1907 he stated: 'My West passed utterly out of existence so long ago as to make it merely a dream.'

western frontier. The canvas was, in fact, a reworked section from one of Remington's largest and most important cavalry scenes. *The Apaches!* (opposite, below), which achieved the second highest price in the sale, was painted in 1904 and is a classic example of Remington's mature work. Notable for its drama combined with a light-filled, Impressionist palette, *The Apaches!* sold for $2,422,500 (£1,501,950). Other highlights included works by John Mix Stanley and William T. Ranney, two mid-19th century artists recognized for their masterful genre scenes. Stanley's *Blackfeet Card Players* (opposite, above), regarded as one of the artist's finest late works, sold for $1,652,500

(£1,024,550) and Ranney's *Kit Carson*, depicting a legendary hero of the frontier, fetched $1,212,500 (£751,750). Among the strong representation of paintings from the Taos School, bidders competed most actively for E. Martin Hennings's luminescent *Four Riders* (above), which fetched $1,102,500 (£683,550), well above the painting's $250,000–350,000 pre-sale estimate. The outstanding success of The John F. Eulich Collection contributed significantly to the $42,564,275 (£26,389,851) total for the day, the second highest sum for an American Paintings auction, surpassed only by Sotheby's record-setting December 1997 sale, which totalled $42,883,525 (£25,301,280).

MASTERPIECES BY CLAUDE MONET | Charles S. Moffett

Charles S. Moffett is Co-Chairman of Impressionist, Modern and Contemporary Art at Sotheby's.

The pre-sale exhibition of *Bassin aux nympheas et sentier au bord de l'eau* at Sotheby's London was the first time the painting had been on public view for nearly half a century. Its sale price of £19,801,500 ($33,068,505) set a world auction record for the artist and made it the 11th most expensive painting ever sold at auction.

In the spring of 1998 Sotheby's sold two exceptional paintings by Monet. In each case, an extraordinary work commanded a remarkable price. *Le Grand Canal* of 1908 is one of six views of the church Santa Maria della Salute that Monet executed during a visit to Venice in the autumn of 1908. All were painted from the Palazzo Barbaro, where for two weeks Monet and his wife were the guests of Mary Young Hunter, a wealthy American who had been introduced to the Monets in London by John Singer Sargent. The palazzo had been lent to Mrs Young by Mrs Daniel Curtis.

Shortly after the middle of October, Monet and his wife moved to the nearby Grand Hotel Britannia. By then he had already established a fixed work routine, concentrating on four different subjects each day, but limiting himself to two hours for each. The final session of the day was devoted to painting the view towards Santa Maria della Salute from a window of the Palazzo Barbaro between 4.00 and 6.00 pm. Since he painted at the same time every day, the view of the church across the canal became a constant. The variables were the weather, light, atmospheric conditions and, of course, Monet's own mood. While he clearly enjoyed recording and exaggerating particular effects of colour and light, he seems to have painted each work in a particular colour key that is especially evocative. Indeed, the meaning of these paintings seems to be inextricably linked to dominant colours and colour combinations.

The record-setting work that was sold in London on 30th June, *Bassin aux nympheas et sentier au bord de l'eau* of 1900, is also an image from a group with very similar compositions but strong differences in palette and mood. It belongs to the first extended group of paintings that Monet painted of his water garden in Giverny and the Japanese footbridge that stands near the entrance. In 1899–1900, he executed 18 paintings of a small section of the water-lily pond and the Japanese bridge that he had constructed in 1893.

The present work is one of three with virtually identical compositions. Monet's extravagantly beautiful interpretation of the scene is thoroughly convincing because the artist has created an image that is, above all, a consummate work of art. The rhythms of brushwork, touches of red, patterns of foliage and flowers, colour harmonies and dissonances, and the sweeping arc that begins on the path in the foreground and ends on the other side of the bridge elicit comparisons to music.

Like *Le Grand Canal*, the painting both celebrates and transcends its subject. These are images that tell us about very special places but also comment on the extraordinary pleasure of visual experiences. They are paintings that are timeless in their appeal and will continue to enthrall viewers for generations to come.

Le Grand Canal was sold at Sotheby's New York on 13th May 1998 for $12,102,500 (£7,382,525), setting an auction record for a Venetian subject by Claude Monet.

CONTEMPORARY ART AT SOTHEBY'S | Tobias Meyer

The 1997–98 season produced the most successful results in the auction of Contemporary Art at Sotheby's since 1990. An example of the current state of the market can be seen in the sale of Mark Rothko's *No. 14, 1960* (see page 91). The painting had not been seen in public for over 20 years, when it was exhibited at a major retrospective of the artist's work, and its undeniable quality was therefore combined with a rare freshness to the market. Its appearance at Sotheby's in November 1997 was greatly anticipated, and its price was driven up to $5,942,500 (£3,506,075), almost twice the previous auction record for this artist established at the height of the market in 1989.

Buyers in this field are now both informed and selective, but once a work meets their criteria they are prepared to bid to unprecedented levels. This process was witnessed in the price achieved for Andy Warhol's ravishing *Orange Marilyn*, sold at Sotheby's in May.

Warhol based *Orange Marilyn* on a still from the 1952 film *Niagara*, in which the radiant, blond-haired beauty first captured the world's attention. The painting is primarily executed in orange, the most vivid colour in the series of 1964 *Marilyn* portraits.
© The Andy Warhol Foundation/ ARS, New York and DACS London 1998.
™ 1998 Estate of Marilyn Monroe by CMG Worldwide. All rights reserved.

In *Large Interior w11 (after Watteau)*, Lucian Freud captures the peculiar psychological state that animates the assembled group while exposing the solitary character of each sitter. The slope of the floorboards draws the viewer into the room while making the sitters seem to almost tumble out of the picture frame.

Orange Marilyn is one of the most universally recognized, quintessential icons of the artist's oeuvre. It extends beyond the boundaries of Pop Art as a painting that perpetuates and transcends its times. An object of exquisite beauty, it is a testament to the 'star' power of both Marilyn and Warhol – individuals whose very names conjure up fame, glamour and tragedy.

The previous record for a painting by Andy Warhol had been set in 1989 at $4,070,000 for the similar *Red Shot Marilyn* – it was my sense that the present work could exceed that figure, based on its importance and quality. Bidding began with five clients quickly pushing the price up to over $8 million. Two serious collectors then drove it to $17,327,500 (£10,569,775), which set the price achieved at almost four times the previous world record for Warhol, and made *Orange Marilyn* the second most expensive contemporary work of art ever sold.

Remarkable results were also achieved for very different works, such as *Large Interior w11 (after Watteau)* by Britain's greatest living painter, Lucian Freud. A compelling and archetypal piece, it is also the largest picture Freud has created to date and the only deliberate paraphrase of an Old Master to be found in his oeuvre, taking its inspiration as it does from Watteau's *Pierrot Content*. Estimated at $2.5–3.5 million, the painting achieved $5,832,500 (£3,557,825), setting a new auction record for the artist.

In this climate clients are recognizing that the value of a key Warhol, for example, is equivalent to that of a key Picasso. High calibre artists of this century are beginning to be appreciated and priced on a similar level. From this vantage point it remains to be seen what the future season holds but it is clear that there is a huge demand for extraordinary art.

Tobias Meyer is Sotheby's Worldwide Director of Contemporary Art.

THE LIVINEC–VALADIER COMMODES | Mario Tavella

Mario Tavella is a Senior Director and Head of the French and Continental Furniture department, Sotheby's London.

The Livinec–Valadier Commodes made for Prince Marcantonio IV Borghese, by Yves Livinec, the mounts by Luigi Valadier, Roman, c. 1784, 101 by 163 by 79 cm (39¾ by 64¼ by 31⅛ in).

Detail of one of the square handles, which appear on each side of the commodes.

The £1.1 million paid in London on the 10th June 1998 for a pair of neo-classical Roman commodes set three new records for the highest worldwide bid at an auction of European continental furniture in the 1997–98 season, the highest price ever paid at auction for furniture executed in Rome, and the highest price for any Italian commodes. These clearly demonstrate a revival of interest in the art market for Italian furniture.

The provenance and craftsmanship of the Livinec–Valadier commodes justify this success. The pair, for which a detailed bill exists dated 19th November 1784, were executed by the French-born ébéniste Yves Livinec (c. 1734–97), with mounts by Luigi Valadier (1726–95), the most celebrated Italian silversmith and bronze-founder of the 18th century. Valadier's prestigious clientele included the Duke of Northumberland, the Cardinal Duke of York, Madame du Barry, the Odescalchi and Chigi families, and Pope Pius VI. It therefore comes as no surprise that Rome's wealthiest collector and most influential prince, Marcantonio IV Borghese (1730–1800), should have commissioned these commodes, in all probability for the Palazzo Borghese. A further pair, of identical design but using different ornaments and materials, were delivered at the same time to his Villa al Pincio.

Modernization of the palazzo and villa commenced at the beginning of the 1770s under the direction of Antonio Asprucci and, as art-historian Professor González-Palacios has suggested, it is possible that he also supervised the overall design of the commodes.

The tops of the present pair are quarterly veneered with verde antico, echoing the extensive use of marble in Rome, and are bordered with a partially gilt-metal border, as was the fashion reserved for the best pieces of furniture of the city's palazzi. The satinwood veneer is delicately inlaid with vegetal motifs in contrasting woods. The pure geometry of the overall shape is emphasized by four stylish, almost minimalist, copper roundels encircling the keyholes and two square handles, whose strikingly modern design is recorded in a drawing attributed to Valadier. The pristine condition of the commodes and their reappearance on the market for the first time in two centuries, combined with their elegance and history, explain the great interest shown by collectors worldwide. Nevertheless, compared with the high prices now commanded by the best French or English furniture, these Italian commodes represent extraordinary value for money and should prove to be a wise investment for the future.

THE WARWICK TABLES

Joseph Friedman

RIGHT The Warwick Tables, a pair of giltwood and lacquer pier tables, supplied to Queen Anne for St James's Palace *c.* 1704–05, by the royal cabinet-maker Gerrit Jensen in association with Thomas Pelletier.

BELOW The cypher of Queen Anne composed of the letters *AR* (Anna Regina), surmounted by the royal crown.

T his outstanding pair of giltwood and lacquer tables commissioned by Queen Anne, which are among the few major pieces of English royal furniture to be auctioned in recent times, sold at Sotheby's in London on 10th July 1998, realizing a price of £1,651,500 ($2,691,945). The result contributed to a total of £5,904,290 ($9,683,036), making this Sotheby's most successful English Furniture sale ever.

The tables bear Queen Anne's cypher and it is probable that they were intended for the Queen's personal use in her private apartments at St James's Palace, her principal residence. They are listed in the palace's furnishing accounts in 1704–05, being among the items supplied that year by Gerrit Jensen, who charged a total of £44. The leading furniture-maker of his day, Jensen served as 'Cabinet Maker in Ordinary' to William and Mary, as well as Queen Anne. It is virtually certain that he produced the tables in association with the carver and gilder Thomas Pelletier, who was also 'Cabinet Maker in Ordinary' to the Queen.

The tables remained in the Royal Collection after Queen Anne's death, and by the early 1800s had been installed in the Ball Room at Hampton Court Palace. They were then removed, presumably at the time of George IV's remodelling of the palace in the 1820s, and passed into the collection of the 3rd Earl of Warwick at Warwick Castle, being listed in an inventory drawn up after his death in 1853. The tables were almost certainly a gift from George IV, whom the Earl served as Lord of the Bedchamber and Lord Lieutenant.

Fully documented through almost 300 years of history, the Warwick Tables are among the greatest treasures of the tradition of patronage and collecting in England.

Joseph Friedman is a Senior Director and Head of the English Furniture department, Sotheby's London.

Kevin Tierney and **Ian Irving** are both Senior Vice Presidents and Heads of the Silver department, Sotheby's New York.

On 24th November 1740, Meissonnier's two tureens were added to the pantry inventory of Evelyn Pierrepont, 2nd Duke of Kingston (1712–73). The clerk simply noted the number of pieces, the weights and their value in French currency. However, their arrival in England must have caused a sensation, they were so advanced stylistically, technically and conceptually that they would have seemed from a different world than that which produced the 3,000 oz. wine cistern made for the 1st Duke by Philip Rollos. Yet, as the cistern was a masterpiece of the baroque, so Meissonnier's tureens were masterpieces of the new genre *pittoresque*. They had been ordered in 1734 by the young Duke, who had been welcomed into Parisian society during his stay in France. It was through such connections, presumably, that he was introduced to his suppliers.

Juste-Aurèle Meissonnier was born in Turin in 1695 to a family of goldsmiths who were originally from Aix-en-Provence. By 1715 he was in Paris, where he quickly received royal patronage, becoming goldsmith by royal privilege in 1724 and Dessinateur de la Chambre du Roi in 1726. He also worked as an *'architectte'* and it was as such that he signed his creations for the Duke. The date letters and discharge marks (1735–38) on the silver reveal that they took at least three years to complete. The tureens also bear the stamped makers' marks of Henry Adnet and Pierre-François Bonnestrenne, indicating that Meissonnier used outside workshops to execute them. A gold and lapis lazuli box, made in 1728 for the widow of Charles II of Spain, is the only known piece to survive stamped with Meissonnier's maker's mark.

The Duke's commission is represented in a signed drawing by Meissonnier and an engraving by Huquier (below) as consisting of two tureens flanking a centrepiece, which appears never to have been executed. The tureens are modelled as barnacle-encrusted shell-form vessels laden with seafood, game and vegetables, the ingredients of the ragoût within. This detailed naturalism, partly cast from life, is arranged in a composition of spiralled movement and sweeping asymmetry and is finished with reflective and matte-chased surfaces. Confident to the point of arrogance, Meissonnier flaunts his genius in bringing his silver to a superb interpretation of the rococo.

The Duke's colourful wife Elizabeth Chudleigh was convicted of bigamy after his death and fled to Russia, taking these and other treasures with her. She died in a newly acquired mansion near Fontainebleau shortly before the French Revolution. The tureens stayed in Russia until they were sold at a Paris auction to J. Seligmann, an agent for J. P. Morgan, in 1909. They reappeared at Christie's in Geneva in 1977 where they sold for $1,104,000, an auction record at that time. One became the property of the Cleveland Museum of Art, the other joined the collection of Baron Thyssen-Bornemisza de Kaszon. The latter was sold at Sotheby's New York on 13th May 1998 for $5,722,500 (£3,490,725), the second highest price ever paid at auction for a piece of silver. It takes its place in history as one of the most expensive works of art ever to be sold on the auction block.

LEFT Meissonnier's proposal for a large *Surtout* and two tureens for the Duke of Kingston, engraved by Huquier.

OPPOSITE The Tureen, Cover and Plateau made for the Duke of Kingston by Juste-Aurèle Meissonnier.

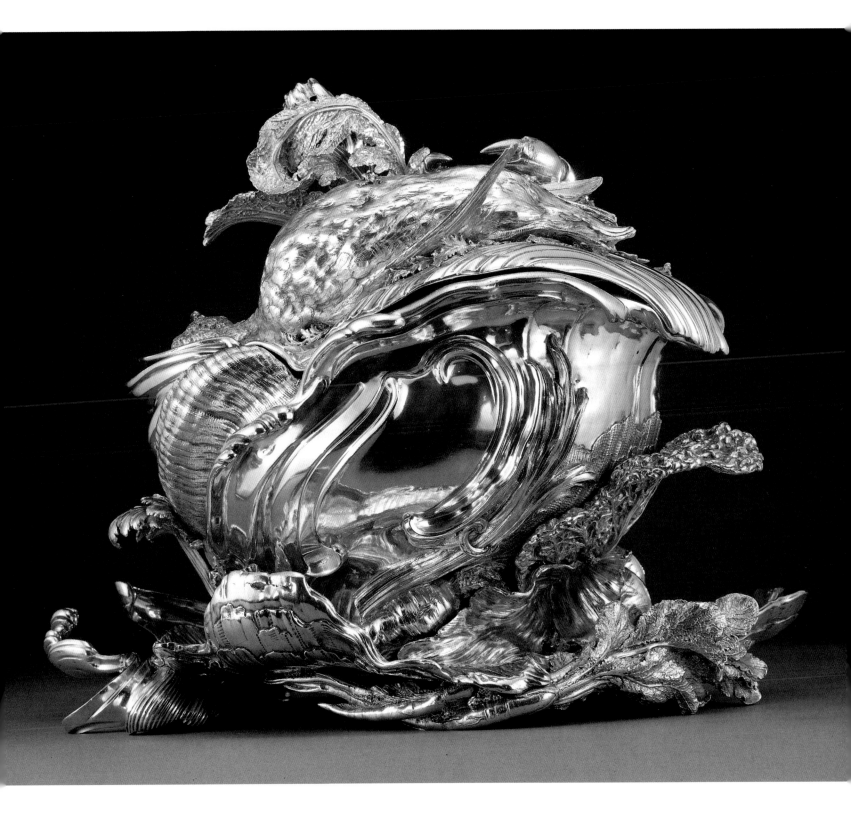

THE STANLEY PAUL SAX COLLECTION OF AMERICANA | Leslie Keno

One of the most notable recent events in the Americana market was the January sale of Mr and Mrs Stanley Paul Sax's Collection of American Furniture and Decorative Arts. It was a great privilege to have known Stan Sax, and the collection he assembled remains a testament to his refined 'eye', exquisite taste and keen interest in American history.

The furniture in the Sax Collection consisted mainly of high-style examples made in the major centres of design and craftsmanship, including Philadelphia, Boston, Salem, New York and Newport. Particularly impressive was the suite of a Philadelphia Chippendale scroll-top companion high chest of drawers and dressing table (above). Stan's reunion of these pieces after decades of separation is one of the great coups in the history of Americana collecting.

The suite, which sold at Sotheby's for $1,212,500 (£739,629), is a masterpiece of the Philadelphia Rococo school, exhibiting the aesthetic heights scaled by the carvers Nicholas Bernard and Martin Jugiez. These men were also responsible for carving the General John Cadwalader Chippendale mahogany hairy-paw-foot wing armchair which sold at Sotheby's in 1987 for $2.75 million (£1,785,714), a world auction record for a piece of furniture at that time.

The four Charles Apthorp family Queen Anne compass-seat side chairs from the collection are perhaps some of the most important examples of colonial seating furniture in existence. The set represents the pinnacle of sophisticated chair design in America during the first half of the 18th century. Each is in remarkable condition, retaining an old finish and their original slip seat cushion frames, which no doubt contributed to their price of $967,000 (£589,870), setting a world record for a set of American chairs.

ABOVE, LEFT The Chippendale carved and figured mahogany scroll-top high chest of drawers and companion dressing table, united by Stanley Paul Sax.

ABOVE The great room in the Stanley Paul Sax residence, Bloomfield Hills, Michigan.

OPPOSITE A view of the Salon.

The sale also featured several examples of Philadelphia seating furniture, including a Chippendale upholstered wing armchair, with dramatically raked-back rear legs and substantial cabriole legs ending in claw-and-ball feet, which achieved $310,500 (£189,405).

Among the side chairs from this region was a Chippendale walnut example, which achieved $122,500 (£68,625). This chair appears to belong to a well-known set of six side chairs and one armchair that was made for the Loockerman family of Dover, Delaware, and is now in the collection of the Diplomatic Reception Rooms of the US Department of State.

Also in the collection were a number of American clocks such as the important Jacob Godshalk tall-case clock from Philadelphia, one of Stan's most prized possessions. This extraordinary piece sold for $442,500 (£269,925).

Among the tables in the collection was the magnificent Van Vechten family Chippendale five-leg gaming table made in New York, c. 1770, which sold for $266,500 (£162,565). Designed for card playing, it boasts an undulating serpentine gadrooned frieze and elegant foliate and asymmetrical C-scroll carving on the knees of the front legs.

The sale also included the Derby family Federal carved and figured mahogany serpentine-front chest on chest, which sold for $178,500 (£108,885) and is one of only five examples of its type attributed to Samuel McIntire. The original owner of this piece was Elias Hasket Derby, who lived in what is considered to be the most expensive Federal house ever built in America.

With highlights such as these, the Stanley Paul Sax Collection is proof that sophisticated collectors in the Americana field are willing to bid vigorously for extraordinary pieces.

Leslie Keno is Senior Vice President and Head of the American Furniture department, Sotheby's New York.

THE COLLECTION OF HRH THE DUKE AND THE DUCHESS OF WINDSOR

C. Hugh Hildesley

C. Hugh Hildesley is Executive Vice President of Sotheby's North and South America.

For those of us who had experienced the sale of the Jacqueline Kennedy Onassis Estate, that of the Windsor Collection exhibited familiar features, not least the sense of actively participating in this century's history. Sotheby's galleries in New York were once again to be transformed. As Labor Day drew near, we were ready for the attendance of those who had never been to an auction before, and crowd control ranked high among our concerns. After literally years of preparation, the exhibition was ready with just hours to spare. The flowers were in place, the media about to gather with their paraphernalia, and then…indefinite postponement, caused by the tragic, untimely deaths of Diana, Princess of Wales and Dodi Fayed.

The challenge of summoning afresh that initial enthusiasm was more than met when the exhibition of over 40,000 items finally opened in February 1998, six months later than originally scheduled. And, as the crowds made their way through the beautiful rooms designed to suggest the Paris house itself, it became clear that an extraordinary story had been recreated for the last time with the actual objects that had surrounded this historic couple. Visitors were once more face to face with history, with style, with romance and with royalty, and the magic of this intriguing couple continued to exert its fascination.

When else would Sotheby's offer within the bounds of one sale catalogue, albeit in multiple volumes, a royal despatch box, a 60-year-old slice of wedding cake, the tartan kilt of the Lord of the Isles, a desk upon which an English monarch had abdicated his throne, and a group of stuffed cushions in the form of pugs?

There was indeed something for everyone, from two ivory and steel boot hooks that found a new home for $230 (£140) to a masterpiece of equestrian art, Sir Alfred Munnings's portrait of *HRH The Prince of Wales on 'Forest Witch'*, commanding the record price for the artist of $2,312,500 (£1,410,625). The Duke's childhood

This portrait of Prince Edward of York in his christening robes, July 1894, was the first item from the collection to be offered for sale. It set the tone for the ensuing sessions when it achieved $27,600 (£16,836) against a pre-sale estimate of $2,000–3,000.

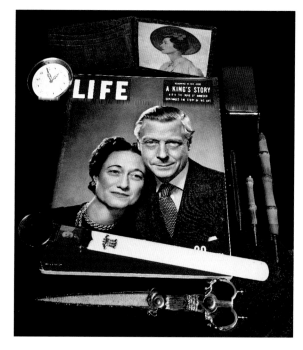

stuffed Chimney Sweep Doll sold for $74,000 (£45,140) against a pre-sale estimate of $800–1,200. This was history with a heart.

As session after session took place, many presided over by Sotheby's Chief Executive, Diana D. Brooks, it became clear that this story had lost none of its power. Bidders vied with each other for just one of the 10,000 photographs, a group of monogrammed linens, a single handbag or a few pairs of gloves. Over 30,000 absentee bidders competed with those in the salesroom, and bids were received from all 50 of the States of the Union and 50 countries.

Once again, the staff at Sotheby's displayed their professionalism at its very best, as the sale surpassed the company's greatest expectations. The total achieved by the sale was $23,362,043 (£14,250,846), the entire net proceeds of which were donated to charity. The next Monday, the spring sale season began and it was 'business as usual'. Only one who does not know Sotheby's would dare suggest that there could never be another sale like this. To those who would venture such a rash statement one can only reply, watch this space….

ABOVE A view of the Windsors' former residence in Paris, including Sir Alfred Munnings's portrait of *HRH The Prince of Wales on 'Forest Witch'*. Painted when the Prince was 27, it captures the aura of patriotic pride that marked his early adulthood.

LEFT These 11 pug pillows had occupied a prominent position in the Duchess's bedroom. Their sale, for a combined total of $37,375 (£22,799), was greeted with an enthusiastic response.

ANCIENT GLASS FROM THE COLLECTION FORMED BY THE BRITISH RAIL PENSION FUND

Richard M. Keresey

Richard M. Keresey is Senior Vice President and Worldwide Head of Antiquities at Sotheby's.

In 1974 the British Rail Pension Fund decided to invest in certain areas of the art market, including ancient glass, using Sotheby's as its primary advisor. One of their first pieces was a Hellenistic glass amphora purchased in 1975 at Sotheby Parke Bernet, New York for $2,500. Further acquisitions resulted in the important British Rail Collection of ancient glass, which was auctioned at Sotheby's London on 24th November 1997. A modest success as an investment, the Hellenistic amphora sold for £3,450 ($5,865), and most of the Fund's later acquisitions fared considerably better.

Although this collection was a corporate investment, it reflected the personal interests of the individuals who had previously owned the pieces. The amphora, for example, had once belonged to Ray Winfield Smith, much of whose collection was in one of my earliest sales in New York in 1975. Like many glass collectors I have known, he had a dynamic personality, a fascinating contrast to the fragile vessels in which he had such an intense interest. Estimating his collection and going

over each piece with him in detail was a memorable experience for a freshman specialist at Sotheby's.

Among the more spectacular vessels in the British Rail collection was a Hellenistic millefiori glass bowl (opposite, top) acquired from Richard Reedy of Gloucester, Massachusetts, whose collection Sotheby's sold in 1979. Purchased then for $55,000, it sold in London 18 years later for £276,500 ($470,000). The simplicity of its form is complemented by the richness of its decoration and colour, and no comparable glass was offered at public auction during that time.

Over half of the British Rail pieces were acquired from Mr and Mrs Andrew Constable-Maxwell, who sold their collection at Sotheby's London in 1979, including a Byzantine glass pitcher (opposite, bottom right). Purchased for £10,000, it sold in 1997 for £17,250 ($29,300). A classic example of its type, it is decorated with Christian symbols produced by blowing the glass into a mould.

The masterpiece of the collection, a Roman Imperial Diatretum (left), was made by an entirely different technique. A tour de force of the glass-maker's art, this vessel is carved from a solid blank of glass and creates the illusion that it is actually two units – a cup suspended within an openwork outer lining. The carving process has been described as requiring 'infinite patience, fanatical concentration, and calm deliberation'. It was acquired in the 1979 sale for £520,000, setting an auction record for ancient glass. In 1997 spirited bidding carried the price up to £2,311,500 ($3,930,000), again establishing an auction record not only for ancient glass, but also for a glass vessel of any period.

A sale of 33 lots in what is to some an obscure field did not seem likely to induce a proverbial 'feeding-frenzy'. So when my colleague Seth Bright and I, with British Rail's consultant Oliver Forge, entered a packed salesroom that November evening, we were uncertain of the outcome. Thus when auctioneer George Bailey brought the hammer down on the last lot, and all 33 items had sold for a total of £3,632,400 ($6,138,756), £650,000 over the high estimate, we felt not only relief, but also a measure of pride. It was a satisfying conclusion to a 22-year process, and a memorable day.

RIGHT Dating from the late 3rd to 2nd century BC, this Hellenistic glass bowl is decorated with opaque yellow and green spiral-shaped canes set in a dark blue matrix.

BELOW, RIGHT This pale green glass bucket, c. AD 5th century, was found in an Anglo-Saxon cemetery on the Longmeadow Estate, Bury St Edmunds, Suffolk. It sold for £205,000 ($346,450).

BELOW, FAR RIGHT Hexagonal glass jugs decorated with Jewish or Christian symbols, such as this example from the early 7th century AD, are thought to have been used as containers for holy oil by the Christians and for oil or some other substance by the Jews for funerary offerings. They were sold to pilgrims in Jerusalem.

OPPOSITE Cage-cups or 'vasa diatreta' (cut vessels), as they were known in the 19th century, were the most expensive form of glassware manufactured during the Roman period and were owned by only the very wealthiest of Roman society. This example has been dated to c. AD 300 and measures 10 by 18.2 cm (4 by 7⅛ in).

Carlton C. Rochell, Jr is Senior Vice President and Head of the Asia Division, Sotheby's North America.

Since its inauguration in 1992 at Sotheby's New York, Asia Week has proved to be a highly successful concept, greatly invigorating the Asian art market in both North America and Europe. Held each March and September in New York, the week provides Sotheby's international clients with a unique opportunity to visit the auction house at a time when every gallery is focused on this diverse collecting field. Collectors and connoisseurs can simultaneously view the exhibitions of works of art from India, Southeast Asia, China, Japan and Korea, attend lectures by distinguished scholars, meet Sotheby's specialists in the field, and take part in other exciting events that accompany the auctions. In 1998 Sotheby's expanded Asia Week to include the London sales of Asian art, so that European clients can attend auctions within a similarly stimulating environment each June.

The 1997–98 auction season was a record year for Asian Art at Sotheby's New York and was highlighted by several important collections, including single-owner sales of Korean Art from the Estate of Marcus W. Scherbacher Family Trust, The Gerry P. Mack Collection of Important Chinese Snuff Bottles, The C. C. Wang Family Collection of Important Chinese Paintings, and Japanese Inro from the Collection of the Late Charles A. Greenfield. A number of outstanding works of art from the Estate of Earl Morse were offered in the March 1998 Asian art sales, including his Gupta red sandstone head of Buddha (see page 122), which brought more than $1 million (£0.6 million), a world record for an Indian stone sculpture at auction.

Another record in the category of Indian and Southeast Asian Art was set in the autumn sale when a Sino-Tibetan gilt-bronze figure of the Dharmapala Mahakala, *c.* 17th century, sold for $387,500 (£240,250, below). This record was subsequently broken in our spring sale when a 15th-century sculpture of Mahakala fetched $690,000 (£414,000, see page 123). The market for Chinese works of art has been equally buoyant, and an Imperial 'famille-rose' peach dish was

Mahakala is one of the most popular and frequently depicted tantric deities in Tibet. As here, he is typically portrayed as a ferocious divinity, but as a guardian his fierceness is only utilized in order to ward off potential harm and protect his devotees, hence his popularity.

sold for $189,500 (£117,490) in September (left). In the same sale, a rare set of 'famille-verte' month cups of the Kangxi period brought $706,500 (£438,030, see page 125), clearly demonstrating the strength of the New York market for fine Chinese ceramics. The results of the first Asia Week in London, held in June 1998, were also extremely positive and ended the year on a strong note. Among the many highlights was a rare *sancai* glazed caparisoned Fereghan Horse, Tang dynasty (below) and a 'Tobacco-leaf' dinner service, which achieved a world record for a single Chinese Export dinner service (see page 124).

The 1997–98 season was an extraordinary year for Asia Week at Sotheby's, particularly with New York seeing the highest total ever realized during the spring sales. Records were set in individual collecting categories, and the number of new buyers continued to increase as clients become intrigued by the sublimely beautiful works of art from Asia and the outstanding artistic qualities that they exemplify.

This Imperial 'famille-rose' peach dish, seal mark and period of Qianlong, measures 20.6 cm (8⅛ in) in diameter. It was sold at Sotheby's New York on 23rd September 1997.

Measuring 70.5 cm (27¾ in) in height, this magnificent Fereghan Horse is of an exceptional size and is also notable for its elaborate trappings and fine *sancai* glazes. It sold for £243,500 ($396,905) at Sotheby's London on 16th June.

A PRIVATE TREATY SALE:
THE SHERBORNE MISSAL

Christopher de Hamel

Dr Christopher de Hamel FSA is a Senior Director and Head of the Western Manuscripts department, Sotheby's Europe.

O n Wednesday 1st July 1998 the supreme Sherborne Missal was finally acquired by the British Library from the Duke of Northumberland. Negotiations on behalf of the Duke were conducted by Sotheby's. The transfer was partly in payment of tax and was the largest such transaction ever to take place in Britain. It was also by far the most expensive illuminated manuscript ever sold, either by auction or by private treaty.

The Sherborne Missal is certainly the finest English gothic manuscript in existence and was, until its sale, probably the most valuable book in private hands. It is a gigantic volume of 536 leaves, approximately 53.6 by 38 cm, comprising the services of the Mass for use in the chapel of the Benedictine Abbey of St Mary, at Sherborne in Dorset, Southwest England.

Its importance is twofold. It is of quite extraordinary richness of illumination, with well over a thousand miniatures and borders throughout. These include portraits of the kings of England and the benefactors of Sherborne Abbey and a famous series of paintings of birds, with their names in English, which form some of the earliest naturalistic paintings in western art. Secondly, the Sherborne Missal is exceptionally fully documented. It includes portraits of its two patrons, Richard Mitford, bishop of Salisbury 1396–1407, and Robert Bruyning, abbot of Sherborne 1385–1415. They probably jointly paid for it. The arms of Henry V occur in the manuscript as Prince of Wales, a title accorded to him in 1400, and those of France are in the ancient form abandoned around 1406. The manuscript is therefore datable to 1396–1407 at the absolute outside, and perhaps between 1400 and 1406.

The manuscript is signed four times by the scribe, the Benedictine monk John Whas. His own portrait appears in the illumination at least three times. The huge manuscript has approximately 40,000 lines of text, and it is no surprise that John Whas records in one inscription that he had to rise early in the morning to labour so hard and that his body was all emaciated with effort. The principal artist was John Siferwas (1360/65–c.1430), a Dominican friar, who signed his name many times. He is one of the earliest English

ABOVE A page from the daily order of service, in which Christ is depicted in an initial letter *I*, showing two apostles and the land of milk and honey. In the margin the patron Robert Bruyning kneels beneath God the Father.

LEFT A marginal detail of a robin from the Canon of the Mass.

A detail from the order of service for the Fourth Sunday in Advent. A wren carries a scroll, drawing attention to the image of Moses and Aaron before Pharoah. The Benedictine scribe, John Whas, is depicted next to the initial *M* containing the image.

artists whose name is known and for whom some body of work survives. There is even a naturalistic self-portrait of him in another British Library manuscript, Harley MS.7026. His name and portrait appear many times in the Sherborne Missal. On one page he quotes his motto, '*God sende vs ryt goud grace*', and paints his own coat-of-arms beside that of the Prince of Wales.

The Missal was still in England when Sherborne Abbey was suppressed under Henry VIII in 1539. It was probably smuggled to France, for the possession of such 'papist' service books became illegal in Protestant England. The manuscript is next recorded in 1703 when it was given by Léonor-François Goyon de Matignon, bishop of Lisieux, 1677–1714, to Nicolas-Joseph Foucault (1643–1721). He, in turn, sold it to Charles d'Orléans (1691–1744), abbé de Rothelin, in whose sale in Paris in 1746 it realized 1,810 livres to Selle, Tresorier

Général de la Marine. It was probably brought back to England in 1787, perhaps by Charles-Alexandre de Calonne (1734–1802), former controller-general of finance under Louis XVI. In February 1800 it appeared at auction in London, 'being the genuine library of George Galwey Mills, Esq. (gone to the West Indies)', lot 1459, and realized £215, then the highest price ever paid in England for any manuscript. The buyer was the second Duke of Northumberland (1742–1817).

Since 1983 the Sherborne Missal has been on loan to the British Library and has usually shared a double-sided glass case with the Lindisfarne Gospels. Now finally the Missal has entered the national collection forever. The sale was concluded in the very week of the official opening by HM The Queen of the magnificent new British Library building in Euston Road, where the Sherborne Missal is now on view.

'SUE', A *TYRANNOSAURUS REX* SKELETON

David Redden

David Redden is Executive Vice President of the Books department, Sotheby's New York.

The high prairie grasslands of South Dakota are carved by the waters of mid-continental streams. One such stream, the Moreau River, cut through the ranch of Maurice Williams and formed a canyon, the exposed walls or buttes of which became a panorama of Earth's geological history. On 12th August 1990, Sue Henrickson, a dinosaur hunter and archaeologist, carefully examined the butte and discovered 'Sue', the largest, most complete and best-preserved example of that most notorious of dinosaurs, *Tyrannosaurus rex*.

What began for Sue Henrickson's colleagues at the Black Hill Institute as a wildly exciting discovery soon became a nightmare of adversarial claims as the Federal Government and the judiciary strove to decide who owned the bones. Ultimately, 'Sue' was awarded to Mr Williams, held in trust for him by the US Government.

However, the process by which 'Sue' might be transferred to appropriate ownership had not been resolved. Here, Mr Williams and the Government turned to Sotheby's. It is true that Sotheby's sells the best of things, and it is true that the auction process can be used to determine and to enhance value. But no one had ever sold a fossil of this importance, a scientific treasure that needed the right home. If Sotheby's were to take on the project, it would be a test of the auction house and of the auction process. We took it on.

An 'air ride' truck was dispatched to haul 'Sue' to New York. Over many months we inventoried rock-encrusted bones, still in their plaster jackets from the excavation site, and fragments nestled in cotton wool. And we worked with palaeontologists to decipher the dinosaur's life story – the battles with other T-rexes and the ravages of disease.

The sale itself comprised one lot and lasted eight minutes. The estimate had been $1,000,000+ and there were a remarkable number of bidders, up to two dozen. Wonderfully, the final bidder was identified as the Field Museum of Chicago, one of America's greatest natural history museums. The purchase price of $8,362,500 (£5,184,750) represented a record many times over, and a new way of buying, as the Field had been supported by organizations including The McDonalds Corporation and The Walt Disney Company.

More than anything it was the skull, as big as a dining room table, that conveyed the character of 'Sue', and the 'grin', filled with dozens of foot-long teeth serrated like steak knives.

FINE ARTS

Rembrandt Harmensz. van Rijn
Portrait of a Bearded Man in a Red Coat
Signed and dated
Rembrandt. fec/ 1633
Oil on oval oak panel,
63.5 by 50.8 cm (25 by 20 in)
New York $9,077,500
(£5,537,275) 30.1.98

The early 1630s were fruitful years for Rembrandt and marked the beginning of a decade of great activity and public achievement. The artist was residing in Amsterdam, having moved there from Leiden in 1631, and was in great demand as a portraitist. Oval portraits, such as the present work, seem to have been in vogue at this time. The painting last appeared on the art market in 1930, and its whereabouts since then had been unknown.

Johannes Cornelisz. Verspronck

Portrait of Andries Stilte as a Standard Bearer
Dated 1640
Oil on canvas, 101.6 by 76.2 cm (40 by 30 in)
New York $1,652,500 (£1,008,025) 30.1.98

Although the identity of the flamboyantly dressed and self-confident sitter in this portrait has been established, little else is known about him. Andries Stilte was born in Haarlem, the same town in which Verspronck lived and worked, and died around 1675. The standard he bears is indicative of the high position he held in a civic militia company called the Kluveniersdoelen. This position was forfeited upon his marriage to Eva Reyniers in 1640, the date of this painting. Verspronck seems to have been something of the family painter. In 1636, he executed a portrait of Stilte's brother and another portrait of Andries.

David Teniers the Younger
*An Elegant Company
Before a Pavilion in an
Ornamental Garden*
Signed and dated DAVID
TENIERS.FEC./1651
Oil on canvas, 70 by 87.6 cm
(27½ by 34½ in)
London £1,101,500
($1,850,520) 3.XII.97

This elegant assembly of
figures in a park is likely to be
a portrait group, and may
represent a particular event,
possibly a wedding. The
picture is dated 1651, the year
in which Teniers moved with
his family from his native
Antwerp to take up a position
as Court Painter in Brussels.

It is probable that the picture
was painted for one of the
local aristocracy there. Its
subsequent provenance is
particularly distinguished
and includes four members
of the Rothschild family.

Sir Peter Paul Rubens
The Head of John the Baptist Presented to Salome
Oil on oak panel, 94 by 101.8 cm (37 by 40⅛ in)
New York $5,502,500
(£3,336,525) 30.1.98

Rubens left for Italy in 1600 a little-known but well-trained master in the Antwerp guild; by his return eight years later he was an internationally renowned artist. Within nine months he was named Court Painter to the Spanish Regents governing Flanders, the Hapsburg Archdukes Albert and Isabella. The Archdukes recognized Rubens's abilities, seeing him as the perfect instrument for their aspirations to move the region into the mainstream of European culture. This recently discovered picture is one of the earliest works painted by Rubens after his return. Since it appears in the Spanish Royal Inventories in 1666, less than 60 years after it was painted, it is possible that the painting was ordered by one of the many Spaniards who came through Antwerp during the city's economic and artistic revival.

**Jacob Isaacksz.
van Ruisdael**

*Winter Landscape with a
Frozen Canal, Farmhouses
and Windmill Beyond*
Signed *JvR* (in ligature) *uisdael*
Oil on canvas, 39.4 by
43.8 cm (15½ by 17¼ in)
New York $1,322,500
(£806,725) 30.1.98

No artist better evokes the
bleakness of winter than
Ruisdael. Around 25 in
number, his depictions of this
season are all on a relatively
small scale and were probably
painted sometime during the
late 1660s and early 1670s.
Executed while the artist was
living in Amsterdam, they are
not representations of actual
places but are intended to
suggest a state of mind. The
paintings are sparse with a
relatively unremarkable
landscape of a few bare trees
and buildings. A small
number of figures provide
whatever animation the
paintings have but, for the
most part, the series is about
the melancholy emptiness of
winter. While many of these
landscapes suggest an
element of tragedy, this
painting has a lighter note
and the clearing sky foretells
an end to the winter months
and the rejuvenation that
comes with spring.

Salomon van Ruysdael

An Extensive River Landscape
Signed with monogram and
dated *SVR 1644*
Oil on canvas, 62 by 91 cm
(24½ by 36 in)
London £2,311,500
($3,883,320) 3.XII.97
From the Henle Collection

With its delicate, silvery
tonality and atmospheric sky,
this is one of the finest works
of the artist's maturity. The
composition of this river
landscape is typical of
Ruysdael's work in the mid to
late 1640s. The bank recedes
on a diagonal to the right,

paralleled in the sky by the
horizontal brushstrokes of
the clouds conducting the
eye towards the horizon at
the extreme right, and the
trees lean out from the bank
over the water.

Bernardo Strozzi
The Incredulity of St Thomas
Oil on canvas, 89 by 98 cm
(35 by 38½ in)
London £1,321,500
($2,167,260) 9.VII.98

Strozzi produced a number
of versions of this New
Testament scene; that
shown here is one of the
later, more mature versions.
This striking composition
has been given a horizontal
emphasis, with Christ turned

towards the viewer, making
St Thomas's gesture the
immediate focal point of
the piece. It has been
suggested that, in making
his choice of subject matter,
Strozzi may have been aware
of the celebrated painting of

the same scene by
Caravaggio, executed in
Rome in 1599 and now in
Potsdam. Although Strozzi
is not known to have visited
Rome, he may have seen a
contemporary copy in his
native Genoa.

Jusepe de Ribera, called Lo Spagnoletto
Girl with a Tambourine
Signed and dated 1637
Oil on canvas, 59 by 45 cm
(23¼ by 17¾ in)
London £1,816,500
($3,051,720) 3.XII.97

'Rude, robust and rugged' is how Martin Soria described this portrait, which he considered one of Ribera's greatest achievements in the art of characterization. More than simply a portrait, it is also a personification of the sense of hearing. It was through an earlier series of the five senses that Ribera had established his reputation in Italy. The paintings in that series are realistic and strongly tenebrist in character and demonstrate a novel and unconventional treatment of their subject matter. What prompted the artist to return to the theme is unknown and the ensuing series, of which this painting is one, is incomplete.

Gaspar van Wittel, called Vanvitelli
View of the Piazza del Popolo, Rome
Signed and dated
:Cas:Van/Wittel/171 – Roma
Oil on canvas, 57.8 by
109.2 cm (22¾ by 43 in)
New York $1,652,500
(£1,008,025) 30.1.98

Gaspar van Wittel (later Italianized to Vanvitelli) was the first Dutch landscape painter to enter the mainstream of artistic life in Italy. In spite of the fact that so many Dutch artists came to Rome in the first half of the 17th century, few found patrons there or sold their works; most of the output of these artists was sent back to

Holland where it found a far more receptive market. It took Vanvitelli's arrival in Rome in c. 1674–75 and the development of an innovative topographical approach to landscape to create a local demand for his pictures. The present view shows the piazza that travellers from the north first encounter when arriving in Rome.

OPPOSITE

Giovanni Antonio Canal, called Canaletto
Venice, The Molo from the Bacino di San Marco with the Piazzetta and the Palazzo Ducale; Venice, the Grand Canal Facing East from the Campo di San Vio
A pair, both oil on canvas, each: 48.5 by 80.5 cm
(19¼ by 31½ in)
London £5,061,500
($8,503,320) 3.XII.97

These pictures were painted early in Canaletto's career, probably in the late 1720s, during the decade when he produced many of his most celebrated works. It was at this time that his ability to portray the light and atmosphere of his native city and to render the texture of the weathered buildings lining the canals found its fullest expression. Certain

features of the Palazzo Barbarigo, visible to the right of *The Grand Canal Facing East*, help to establish a dating for this pair of paintings.

Jean-Honoré Fragonard
'La coquette'
Inscribed *Frago*, red chalk
over fine indications in
black chalk, 37.9 by 24.7 cm
(14¾ by 9¾ in)
New York $310,500
(£189,405) 28.1.98

This drawing belongs to a
group of red chalk studies of
young women apparently
made by Fragonard over a
period of about ten years,
between 1775 and 1785. The
identity of the model has
been much debated, with the
artist's famously delightful
sister-in-law, Marguerite
Gérard, and his daughter,
Rosalie, both having their
supporters. There is
considerable stylistic
variation among Fragonard's
studies of this type; here,
the chalk used is a dark
vermilion colour. Attention
is entirely focused on the
grace of the figure and the
crisp, reflective shimmer of
the silk dress, without the
distraction of background
detail. The combination of
the skillful use of the chosen
medium to create effects of
light, and the manner in
which the drawing appears
to float on the paper is
reminiscent of similarly
virtuoso studies in pen and
ink by Giambattista Tiepolo.

Hans Holbein the Younger
Tantalus
Inscribed in black ink
TANTALUS, pen and black
ink and watercolour,
heightened with gold,
diameter 5.1 cm (2 in)
New York $745,000
(£454,450) 28.1.98

Although the most generally
familiar of Holbein's
drawings are his portraits,
and in particular the great
series representing Henry
VIII and members of his
court now in the Royal
Collection at Windsor Castle,
numerically the greatest part
of his oeuvre consists of
designs for the decorative
arts – stained glass, jewellery
and goldsmiths' work.
Many of these drawings
appear to have been made
for Henry VIII during
Holbein's second residence
in England (1532–43) and it
seems probable that the
present drawing, 'a
miniature masterpiece',
shares these origins.

Jusepe de Ribera, called Lo Spagnoletto
Study of the Head of a Man
Point of the brush and two
shades of pinkish-red wash,
25.2 by 18 cm (9⅞ by 7⅛ in)
London £80,700 ($131,541)
8.VII.98

A visit to Naples in 1616
brought Ribera into contact
with the work of Caravaggio
and his followers. The older
painter's style influenced the
development of Ribera's
technique, with its
concentration on dramatic
lighting and the realistic
depiction of its sitters. The
extraordinary technique
suggests a dating in the
late 1620s for this
exceptionally powerful,
almost grotesque, study
of a head.

John Constable, RA
*Harnham Bridge Looking
Towards Salisbury Cathedral*
Oil on canvas, 56 by 77.5 cm
(22 by 30½ in)
London £551,500 ($898,945)
9.VI.98
Property of the Executors of
the late Nicholas Phillips

This important landscape
dates from 1820 during
Constable's longest and
happiest stay in Salisbury. It
was painted at the village of
East Harnham, just south of
the city, from the grounds
of the Rose and Crown Inn
and shows the west side of

the Harnham Bridge, which
was built over the River Avon
by Bishop Bingham, *c.* 1240.
The bridge was constructed
at the point where the river
divides into two; the arches
illustrated here cross over
the wider southern channel.
Constable was a keen

observer of bird life and this
picture includes vivid
depictions of birds in the sky
and swallows skimming
across the water. The
undergrowth in the
foreground and the foliage
by the bridge are rendered
with considerable panache

and in the distance the great
spire of the cathedral rises,
in Constable's words, 'like
a needle'.

John Frederick Herring, Snr
Shoeing Imaum
Signed and dated *J.F.Herring Senr/1856*
Oil on canvas, 122 by 152.5 cm (48 by 60 in)
London £1,046,500 ($1,705,795) 9.VI.98

Shoeing Imaum is one of the finest of Herring's works from the period when he had moved to Meopham Park near Tonbridge in Kent and began to concentrate on genre subjects. In the centre is *Imaum*, the famous Arab horse, originally a gift to Prince Albert from the Imaum of Muscat and the subject of several of Herring's compositions. The figure of the blacksmith was modelled by William Terry who worked for Herring for 17 years until 1856 and appeared in many of his pictures. To the left, bringing in a bowl of soup, is the artist's youngest daughter Jennie. The picture was commissioned by James Merry, a prosperous Scotsman who owned a number of racehorses including *Thormanby*, winner of the Derby and the Ascot Gold Cup and sire of three classic winners. Merry went on to become MP for Falkirk Burghs in 1859 and was christened 'the member for Thormanby' by Disraeli, alluding to his greater fame as a racehorse owner.

John Ferneley, Snr
Ralph John Lambton and his Huntsman and Hounds
Signed and dated *J. Ferneley/ Melton Mowbray/1832*
Oil on canvas, 110 by 156 cm (43¼ by 61½ in)
London £397,500 ($675,750) 12.XI.97
Sold by the Los Angeles County Museum of Art to Benefit Future Acquisitions

Ralph John Lambton and his elder brother William Henry were both dedicated huntsmen. In 1793 William paid 500 guineas to Lord Talbot of Ingestre Hall for a pack of foxhounds that had gloriously long pedigrees, 'as long as political speeches', and became the foundation of the famous Lambton Hounds. Following William's early death in Pisa aged 33, Ralph took over the care of

the pack and, after huntsman James Shelley's death, hunted his hounds himself until 1825, when he had a bad fall and was unable to carry the horn. In 1827 John Winter, his first whip, acted as huntsman and it is he that is shown to the left of the present picture, which was commissioned by the members of the Sedgefield Hunt and presented to Ralph in 1832.

Paul Sandby, RA
Windsor – View of the Round Tower from the Officers' Guard Chamber
Inscribed on mount *by Paul Sandby 1752* and numbered *3946*
Watercolour over pencil heightened with bodycolour, with original wash line border, 31 by 63.5 cm (12 by 25 in)
London £161,000 ($262,430) 16.VII.98

Windsor Castle provided Sandby with the most important material of his career; as Jane Roberts has written, it was 'for Paul Sandby what Venice was for Canaletto'. For half a century, Windsor enabled him to draw the most important views which, because it was the home of the Royal Family, were filled with people from all walks of life. This was a potent and attractive combination for him. In the present watercolour Sandby chose the view looking East from the Guard Room to the Round Tower with the 'Norman' gateway on the left. The recent discovery of this painting adds to the magnificent body of Sandby's work once owned by Sir Joseph Banks, one of the artist's foremost patrons.

Joseph Mallord William Turner, RA
Coastal View at Sunset with Fishing Boat Returning to Port
Watercolour over pencil heightened with bodycolour on blue paper, 19.2 by 27.4 cm (7½ by 10¾ in)
London £164,300 ($274,381)
8.iv.98

This newly discovered watercolour by Turner belongs to a group of sea and cloud studies dated to *c.* 1835, many of which are in the Turner Bequest at the Tate Gallery, London. The watercolours are all on the same blue paper and have the same approximate measurements. The study entitled *Waves Breaking on the Shore* (no. 419) is particularly striking in its similarity to the present work, with the same use of yellowy bodycolour in the sea area and sky, and a blue horizon.

Richard Parkes Bonington
Shipping off Genoa
Watercolour heightened with bodycolour, gum arabic, scratching out and stopping out, 11 by 14 cm (4¼ by 5½ in)
London £98,300 ($167,110)
13.xi.97

Returning from their journey to Italy, Bonington and Charles Rivet travelled to Genoa along the coast from Spezzia on 8th June 1826 and spent two days in the city. The visit is recorded in this watercolour, which also depicts the foothills of the Ligurian Appenines in the distance. A passing rain shower enters the composition from the left, creating movement and countering the abrupt diagonal thrust of the clipper's mast.

VICTORIAN PICTURES

John Frederick Lewis, RA
An Armenian Lady, Cairo –
The Love Missive
Signed and indistinctly dated
J.F. Lewis [185]4
Oil on panel, 46 by 35 cm
(18 by 13¾ in)
London £727,500
($1,222,200) 5.XI.97

That this painting represents
a theme of romantic intrigue
is made clear by the
quotation from Byron that
forms its sub-title: 'The
token-flowers that tell / What
words can never speak so
well'. The young concubine
holds in her lap a posy, the
'love missive' just received
from her admirer. In the
language of flowers, each
bloom carries a particular
message: the roses stand for
love, the pansy – *pensée* – for
thoughts, and the forget-me-
nots for true love. Her eyes
rest on them, and her
expression seems to suggest
that she returns the
sentiments expressed.
Displayed at the Royal
Academy in 1855, this was
Lewis's first work in oil to be
shown in a public exhibition
and, as the *Art Journal*
observed, 'it has all the finish
of his water-colour works,
but with more softness'. It
was much loved by John
Ruskin, who wrote 'no words
are strong enough to express
the admirable skill and
tenderness of pencilling and
perception shown in this
picture'.

Franz Xavier Winterhalter
Jeune fille de l'Ariccia (Young Girl from Ariccia)
Signed and dated *1838*
Oil on canvas, 147.3 by
114.3 cm (58 by 45 in)
New York $1,762,500
(£1,075,125) 23.X.97

A number of Winterhalter's
early paintings, including
this example, were inspired
by his sojourn in Italy from
1832 until 1834. These years
had a profoundly liberating
effect on the artist who, until
then, had been confined
primarily to lithographic
work and the occasional
portrait commission from
Grand Duke Leopold of
Baden. In his only surviving
letter from Rome, written in
March 1833, Winterhalter
expressed his delight with
the country, 'I will be glad all
my life that I came here'. For
the first time he could
embrace subjects he had
never addressed before. In
particular, the seemingly
simple, sensuous lives of the
Italian peasants of the south,
resplendent in local
costume, were a great
inspiration to the young
northern painter in search
of the picturesque.

Sir John Lavery, RA
Playing Golf at North Berwick
Signed
Oil on canvas, 174 by
201.5 cm (68½ by 79¼ in)
London £727,500
($1,222,200) 26.XI.97
Property of the Western Club,
Glasgow

Lavery was an indifferent golfer – an Irish caddy once told him, 'Ah, sir, there are very few who can play like you' – but he quickly recognized golf as a key element in the history of the North Berwick landscape. The central figure teeing off, possibly Lady Astor, is on the 6th hole; to her right lies the island of Fidra. In many ways this painting is a radical departure from the traditional society portrait and exemplifies a genre that Lavery can almost claim to have invented, that of depicting fashionable society at play. The present work is the earliest in a long series by the artist set in such resorts as Cannes, Palm Beach and the great houses of Britain, which epitomize the carefree glamour of the 1920s and '30s. This painting achieved a world auction record for the artist.

Laurence Stephen Lowry, RA
The Regatta
Signed and dated 1949
Oil on canvas, 77 by 102.5 cm
(30¼ by 40¼ in)
London £386,500
($649,320) 26.xI.97
Property from the Collection of the late Rt Hon the Lord Walston, CVO

Set at Edgecroft, this painting is based on a drawing commission by the *Manchester Guardian*. It contains Lowry's distinctive impressions of everyday life continuing against a backdrop of industrial buildings bathed in a white haze; this often presented a disquieting vision of man alienated and impersonalized by industrialization. Here an element of humour and humanity remains in the depiction of the intensely personal life of his subjects.

Walter Richard Sickert, ARA
Vernet's, Dieppe
Signed
Oil on canvas, 61 by 49.5 cm
(24 by 19½ in)
London, £89,500 ($146,780)
10.vI.98

Painted *c.* 1920, *Vernet's, Dieppe* is a major painting from the artist's last period of working in Dieppe. The end of the First World War meant Sickert could again travel to France and he set up home a few miles inland from Dieppe. Upon the death of his wife in 1922 he moved into the town, and the paintings of this time offer a new and distinctive view of the place that was one of the central motifs in the artist's work. Vernet's was situated on the Quai Henri IV on the north shore of the port. It was a popular café: during the day it operated as a bistro catering largely to locals, at night it featured singers and attracted a more cosmopolitan crowd.

William Adolphe Bouguereau

The Grapes (La grappe de raisin)
Signed and dated 1869
Oil on canvas laid down on cradled masonite, 146.1 by 114.3 cm (57½ by 45 in)
New York $1,020,000 (£612,000) 7.v.98

Considered an exceptionally fine example of Bouguereau's early maturity, *The Grapes* was conceived to charm and engage the viewer on many levels. Conceptually related to Raphael's *Madonna of Loreto* in the Louvre, the artist establishes a dialogue with the grand pictorial tradition of the Renaissance with his invention of a secular setting and new arrangements for the figures that relate to the High Renaissance picture but do not copy it. He dazzles the viewer with a display of faultless draughtsmanship and rich but subtle colourations that also recall the French Academy's then two-century long insistence on just such virtues. Simultaneously, Bouguereau engages the viewer emotionally with a new 'heroism of domesticity' which ennobles the theme of maternity to the same level previous academicians had hoped for in history painting. The dramatic use of light and shadow are strongly brought to bear in this service as they also enchant with the sparkle and glint off the maid's headdress and the child's hair.

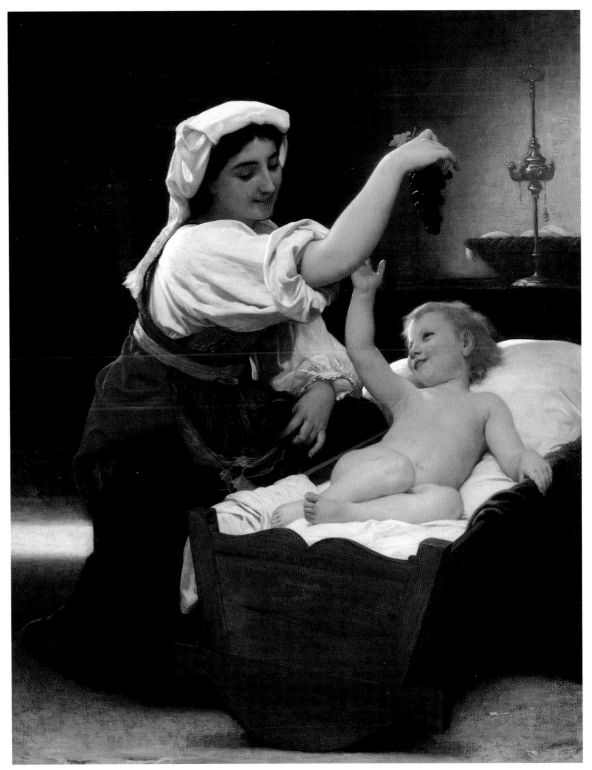

Alfred Stevens
Le salon du peintre
Signed and dated *Paris 1880*
Oil on canvas, 87 by 116.2 cm
(34¼ by 45¾ in)
New York $1,652,500
(£991,500) 7.v.98

By the 1870s Alfred Stevens could claim the patronage of many of the leading European and American collectors, as well as the friendship and esteem of his peers, such as Degas and Manet. The large sums that his paintings commanded enabled Stevens to live in a richly decorated, elegant house in Paris, the salon of which is depicted here. This work now stands as a poignant reminder of vanished grandeur, for, in the year it was painted, Stevens's house was purchased by the city and demolished. *Le salon du peintre* can also be seen as a symbol of the transition of wealth and power from the old world to the new, since it was purchased directly from the painter by William K. Vanderbilt, whose new mansion was rising on Fifth Avenue at 52nd Street. The Indiana limestone building, in the early French Renaissance chateauesque style, transformed the scale and ambition of American domestic architecture and was also the scene of Alva Vanderbilt's successful campaign to become the arbiter of taste in New York and Newport.

OPPOSITE

Francesco Hayez
Rebecca alla fonte (Rebecca at the Well)
Oil on panel, 112 by 85 cm
(44⅛ by 33½ in)
Milan L1,020,775,000
(£335,528; $559,896) 9.vi.98

Rebecca at the Well was executed in 1831 for Gaetano Taccioli, a 'nobile di sentimenti liberali', who commissioned two further paintings from the artist. *Rebecca* marked a turning point in Hayez's oeuvre in its novel use of neutral chromatic tones that were from then on to characterize the painter's palette. It also has in common with other paintings by Hayez the use of a theme as pretext for a sentimental and erotic form of painting. It has been noted that the moving intensity of Rebecca's stare is of a power that goes beyond her biblical identity and gives her an emblematic quality that Hayez continued to develop in subsequent allegories.

Antonio Fabrés y Costa
The Arab Sentinel
1879, signed
Oil on canvas, 164 by 86 cm
(64½ by 34 in)
London £287,500 ($480,125)
24.VI.98

Having moved to Rome in
1875 in order to complete his
sculptural training, Fabrés
became deeply impressed
by the paintings of Mariano
Fortuny and, like Fortuny,
subsequently abandoned his
former discipline. Whilst the
bright colouring of the tiles
and luxurious fabric of the
guard's costume reflect the
artist's mastery of the brush,
his earlier training is
illustrated by the
monumental central figure
and well-balanced
composition. The lantern
and column help to define
the sense of space in the
foreground, which is
softened by the varying
depths of field achieved
by the small group in
the backroom and, in turn,
by the verdant garden
beyond. This work, which
was exhibited to tumultuous
acclaim, represents
Fabrés's first significant
composition depicting
orientalist subject matter.

Joaquin Sorolla y Bastida
Playa de Valencia
1916, signed
Oil on canvas, 47 by 58 cm
(18½ by 22¾ in)
London £320,500 ($535,235)
24.VI.98

By 1916 Sorolla had gained recognition and respect on an international level. He had exhibited in major cities in Europe and America, received prizes and honours from various countries, as well as from his native Spain, and was much in demand as a society artist. This popularity did not prevent him from returning to paint on the beach at Valencia which, from the last years of the 19th century through to the end of his life in 1923, was the central and dominant influence on his painting. Among those executed in 1916 are found 'the most beautiful of his works'. Probably the most striking element of this era is Sorolla's bravura and sophisticated use of brush strokes. The hat of the seated lady on the left of the present work is depicted more by its shadows than by its form, which is not only stunningly effective visually but also, through its levity of touch, complements the air of Belle Époque elegance that the artist successfully conveys.

Mary Cassatt
A Kiss for Baby Anne (No. 3)
1897, signed
Pastel on paper, 43.2 by
64.8 cm (17 by 25½ in)
New York $1,762,500
(£1,092,750) 20.v.98

For almost 25 years Cassatt's primary audience was the Parisian art world. The decision to exhibit in New York in 1898 meant that the first and only response to her latest work would be from Americans. With this in mind, Cassatt devoted most of 1897 to a series of pastels, paintings and prints, of which *A Kiss for Baby Anne*

(No. 3) is one example. Cassatt's choice of model for Anne says much about how she observed American taste from her position as an expatriate in Paris, in that she seems to be striving to depict a child who will be instantly recognizable as 'American'. The most eye-catching passage of the work is the child's glistening hair

that looks like spun gold, capturing a blondness that is essential to the overall message. With its combination of tonal effects, produced by rubbing and layering, parallel hatching to create substance in the bodies, and quick, sharp strokes for the details, this pastel is a tour-de-force of the artist's technique.

Frederic Remington
The Trooper
c. 1891–1902, signed
Oil on canvas, 123.8 by
86.4 cm (48¾ by 34 in)
New York $2,532,500
(£1,570,150) 20.v.98
From the John F. Eulich
Collection

The year 1891 is recognized
by scholars as the apex of
Frederic Remington's career
as a painter of military
subjects. In the decades
that followed, he would
sensitively portray the
landscape of the vanishing
West and create a mythic
stature for the American
cowboy in both paint and
bronze. As a young boy,
Remington grew up idolizing
his father who was a
decorated cavalry officer in
the Civil War. Throughout
his life he would remain a
devotee of American military
life and, although never
formally joining their ranks,
he did become an artist-
correspondent during the
days of the Northern Plains
Indian Wars during which he
witnessed and recorded
much of the action. For an
artist who had specialized
in dramatic depictions of
horses in motion and
military men of valour, *The
Trooper* was a seminal work.
It remains a grand tribute to
the nation's equestrian
military history and to the
cavalry's finest artistic
chronicler.

John Singer Sargent
In the Garden, Corfu
1909, signed
Oil on canvas, 91 by
71.1 cm (36 by 28 in)
New York $8,362,500
(£4,933,875) 3.XII.97

In the late summer of 1909,
Sargent and his sister Emily
embarked on their annual
European excursion, during
which they were joined by
their close friends Jane and
Wilfred de Glehn and Eliza
Wedgwood. By October, the
group had arrived on the
Greek island of Corfu where
they had arranged to stay at
the Villa Sotiriotesa. The
villa's verdant garden
provided the setting for this
painting, Sargent's best
known and most important
work of his two documented
visits to the island. The
central figure in the
composition is Jane Emmet
de Glehn, the American-born
painter whose husband
Sargent had met while
working on the commission
for the Boston Public Library
murals. It is an example of
Sargent's 'painted diaries',
the name given to his
European subject paintings
by his second cousin, Mary
Newbold Patterson Hale:
'Other travellers wrote their
diaries; he painted his'.

Frederick C. Frieseke
White Lilies
c. 1912, signed
Oil on canvas, 71.1 by
91.4 cm (28 by 36 in)
New York $1,652,500
(£1,024,550) 20.v.98

White Lilies was executed
when Frieseke was at the
height of his powers. Writing
to his new dealer, William
Macbeth, in 1912, he spoke of
the canvas as 'the best thing
I have ever done'. Its setting
is a garden in Giverny, where
the Friesekes had been
summering for a number of

years, and the young model
was a professional from Paris
who was known to have
posed for others in the
American colony of artists.
The dazzling direct sunlight
in the painting creates
patterns of light and shadow
across the garden as well as
highlighting those inherent in

the man-made structures of
the chair, shutter and trellis.
The deceptively simple
composition, its elements
arranged and cropped like an
informal snapshot, reveals
the painter's genius in the
way he suggests a multitude
of organizational forces with
the patterns that result.

Georgia O'Keeffe
From the Plains
1919, signed
Oil on canvas, 69.2 by
59.1 cm (27 ¼ by 23 ¼ in)
New York $3,632,500
(£2,143,175) 3.XII.97
Property from the Andrew
Crispo Collection

Georgia O'Keeffe grew up
with a vision of Texas
inspired by the stories her
mother told her as a child.
That vision would be
enriched in later years when
she moved to Amarillo, Texas
in 1912. By the time she
returned to New York in 1919,
the Southwest was deeply
etched in her mind. In
addition to evoking her
auditory memories –
particularly the lowing of
cattle 'loud and raw under
the stars in the wide empty
country', *From the Plains*
embodies O'Keeffe's
reaction to the landscape
of the area, successfully
capturing the awe-inspiring
feeling of space created by an
endless sky rising above a
vast landscape. Colour tinges
this space with a range of
emotions, from the turbulent
cloud topped by red and
angular black forms, which
represent the persistent
sound of the lowing cattle,
to the sweeping blues and
greens of the expanse of
land over which that
sound travelled.

Stuart Davis

Odol

Signed and dated '24
Oil on canvasboard, 61 by
45.7 cm (24 by 18 in)
New York $2,422,500
(£1,429,275) 3.XII.97
Property from the Andrew
Crispo Collection

Odol is a seminal work in
the history of 20th-century
painting and belongs to
a series of still-life
compositions painted by
Davis between 1923 and
1924. These studies of
overscaled everyday objects,
with their hard-edged focus
on popular culture, prefigure
the American Pop Art
movement. The artist's
growing fascination with the
imagery of modern
packaging is emphasized in
this depiction of a popular
brand of mouthwash, as is
the role that brand names
played in the daily lives of the
American public. Davis
isolates the product,
highlighting the brand's
name. The shape of the
bottle is silhouetted against a
checkered motif which,
together with the tilted
transparent form, creates
three spatial planes. The
layered effect achieved is
suggestive of Davis's earlier
collage works.

Circle of Juan Rodríguez Juárez
De español, y de india produce mestiso
c. 1720, inscribed with title
Oil on canvas, 104.1 by 147 cm (41 by 57⅞ in)
New York $123,500 (£72,865)
25.XI.97
From the Barratt-Brown Collection

The pictorial genre known as *castas* (castes) is one of the most compelling artistic manifestations of the Colonial period in Mexico and this work, from a set of five paintings, is among the finest of the type. Caste paintings, popular throughout the 18th century, depict the complexities of race mixing among the three major groups that inhabited the colony during this period: Indian, Spanish and African. Each scene portrays a man and woman of different race with one or two of their progeny and is accompanied by an inscription that identifies the results of racial mixing. In this example the inscription reads, '*De español, y de india produce mestiso*' (Spanish and Indian produce Mestizo). The painting depicts a Spanish man, dressed in fashionable French clothing, with his Indian wife, who is bejewelled and draped in a native cloak, accompanied by their children. In early caste paintings such as this, the assignment of luxurious clothing is meant to demonstrate to the race-obsessed Spaniards that, despite the proliferation of castes in the colony, society remained orderly and prosperous.

Diego Rivera
Nature morte avec géranium
Signed and dated *Sepbre 1916*
Oil and heavy impasto on
canvas, 72.4 by 54 cm (28½
by 21¼ in)
New York $1,102,500
(£650,475) 25.XI.97
From the Barratt-Brown
Collection

Diego Rivera spent the years
1912 to 1921 in Paris, where
he was in communication
with many key figures of the
European avant-garde.
There, he experimented with
a wide variety of Cubist visual
strategies in his art and, by
the year 1916, had derived a
particularly pared-down,
almost rigid manner of
Cubist expression. The
present still life, created in
this critical year, is a visually
daring and intellectually
challenging piece,
embodying elements
representative of Rivera's
distinctive modernist
vocabulary. Of particular
note is the concentration on
the significance of texture,
the harmonization of colour
(with the reds, greens and
whites possibly referring to
the Mexican national
colours), the creation of
dramatic effect through the
depiction of an inky shadow,
and the softening of the
composition's hard edge
with the geranium's leaves
and flowers. *Nature morte
avec géranium* reflects the
fertility of Rivera's
imagination as he struggled
to create something unique,
personal and specifically
Mexican in an international
mode of visual expression.

Joaquín Torres-García
Construcción en blanco y negro
Signed, dated *38 ENE 1* and
inscribed *AAC*
Tempera on board, 81.2 by
102 cm (32 by 40¼ in)
New York $442,500
(£269,925) 27.V.98
From the Rolf and Margit
Weinberg Collection

Painted in 1938, this complex
work comes from a group
that the artist purged of signs
and pictographs found in
previous paintings. By
concentrating on dramatic
shading of forms, and on a
monochromatic palette, the
imagery is anchored more
firmly to the idea of

architecture, symbolizing
order and construction
reminiscent of ancient walls
and the stonecutting of the
Incas, as well as the natural
geology of a cliff wall. This
approach allowed the artist
a larger measure of freedom
in determining the size of
different units, establishing a

range of rhythmically complex
relationships. Joaquín Torres-
García believed that an
aesthetic ordering of this kind
achieved a unity between
Uruguayan culture, which he
cared for passionately, and
universal theories of
abstraction that linked his art
to a European tradition.

Wifredo Lam

Ogue Orisa (Euggue Orissa, L'herbe des dieux)
Signed and dated *1943*
Oil on canvas, 181.9 by
125.1 cm (71⅝ by 49¼ in)
New York $1,322,500
(£793,500) 25.XI.97

During the 1940s, Wifredo Lam executed a series of paintings that reflected his re-acquaintance with forms of Afro-Cuban religious practices. Previously, he had spent a significant amount of time in Europe absorbing, and reinventing, the Cubist and Surrealist models to which he was exposed by friends such as Pablo Picasso, André Breton and Max Ernst, among others. The war in Europe caused Lam to return to the Caribbean. During this period, Lam began to link the artistic experiments he had undertaken in Europe with the impact of the Cuban landscape and his memories of Afro-Cuban religious practices with which he had been acquainted as a child. This work, from what is recognized as the 'heroic' period in his art, incorporates a variety of motifs relating to *santería*, the blending of African and Christian forms of worship. The jungle, dwelling place of the *orishas* (gods and spirits who embodied powers of both good and evil), literally became the theatre of creation of some of Lam's most memorable reflections upon the qualities of the spiritual landscape of both Cuba and Haiti.

Paul Cézanne
Une moderne Olympia
(or *Le pacha*)
c. 1870
Oil on canvas, 56.5 by 55 cm
(22¼ by 21⅝ in)
New York $5,942,500
(£3,506,075) 13.XI.97

In 1865 Manet's *Olympia* was shown at the Salon des Refusés, where it greatly affected Cézanne, staying in his mind until 1870 when he decided to 'update' it and produce a 'modern' version. Manet's knowing courtesan, which had outraged both the public and press, looked back to the nudes of Titian and Goya, treating them with respect and considerable irony. Cézanne's corresponding relationship to Manet, and through Manet to the old masters, whilst highly complicated was clearly a rejection of the contemporary relevance of their solutions to pictorial problems. In attempting to 'outdo' Manet, Cézanne offered an ironic commentary on his sources that still astonishes by its strangeness and modernity. *Une moderne Olympia* was once in the collection of Auguste Pellerin, an early connoisseur of Cézanne's work.

Edgar Degas
Après le bain
1896, signed
Oil on canvas, 77 by 83 cm
(30¼ by 32⅝ in)
New York $6,602,500
(£4,027,525) 13.v.98
Property from the Estate of
Wendell Cherry

From the mid 1880s until his death in 1917, Degas's work became progressively bolder and more innovative, characterized as it was by an increased emphasis on texture and colour, and a general softening of contours, which sometimes verged on the abstract.

During the 1890s he produced a number of large-scale oil paintings of female nudes, three of which, including this example, were based on a photograph entitled *Après le bain*, now in the J. Paul Getty Museum. Jean Sutherland Boggs has asserted that the present

version is 'the one... with the most uncomplicated visual appeal, and the most sensual. The nude gives the greatest sense of her enjoyment of the position she has assumed, her soft flesh caressed by the towel'.

Edvard Munch
Ibsen in the Grand Café
c. 1898
Oil on canvas, 72 by
100.6 cm (28⅜ by 41¾ in)
London £1,761,500
($2,941,705) 30.VI.98
Property from the Estate of
Friederich Kessler

Munch's portrait of Henrick Ibsen seated in the café of the Grand Hotel, Christiania (modern Oslo), is a work of great significance, bringing together as it does two figures who dominated not merely Norwegian cultural life in the second half of the 19th century, but the art and literature of all Europe. The

artist uses a horizontal format to contrast his sitter's imposing features – the only source of light in an otherwise dark interior – with the view through a window to the street beyond. A curtain divides the picture, separating the playwright from his public and blurring the distinction between stage

and reality. To the left Ibsen confronts the viewer in isolation from the mundanities of the world outside; on the right is an evocation of one of the central themes of Ibsen's plays: the hardship and heartache to be found in everyday life. Recalling the playwright, theatre director

Lugné-Poe said: 'I have never been able to forget his eyes, which only the painter Edvard Munch once succeeded in reproducing. One eye, as though half-asleep, reflected and pondered, while the other observed…sharply and with intense and surprising animation and warmth.'

Auguste Rodin

Balzac
Inscribed *A. Rodin*, cast in
1971 by Georges Rudier, 11/12
Bronze, green and brown
patina, height 297.2 cm
(117 in)
New York $3,522,500
(£2,148,725) 13.v.98

'Nothing I have ever done
satisfied me so much,
because nothing cost me so
much, nothing sums up so
profoundly what I believe to
be the secret law of my art,'
said Rodin of this
monumental work, which
was commissioned by the
Société des Gens de Lettres
in 1891. Immersing himself
in Balzacian iconography
and literature, Rodin
gradually moved away from
relatively conventional
studies towards a more
expressive dynamism. His
final version showed the
author 'labouring in his
study, his hair in disorder, his
eyes lost in a dream', draped
in the Dominican robe he
wore when working. Now
recognized as one of Rodin's
greatest works, the sculpture
was mocked by the public
and rejected by the
commissioning body. It was
not until 1927 that the full-
scale figure was cast in
bronze by Alexis Rudier for
the Musée Rodin.

Amedeo Modigliani
Portrait de Baranowski
1918, signed
Oil on canvas, 112 by 56 cm
(43¾ by 21⅝ in)
London £4,291,500
($7,166,805) 30.VI.98
Property of the Robert and
Lisa Sainsbury Charitable
Trust Sold to Establish a Unit
for Japanese Cultural Studies
at the University of East
Anglia

Despite describing himself as a poet and a painter, little is known about Baranowski. As a Polish émigré living in Paris he may have met Modigliani through a fellow countryman, Leopold Zborowski, a book and picture dealer and close friend of the painter. What is certain is that his youthful good looks inspired Modigliani to create one of the most outstanding portraits of his last years, combining the likeness of an individual with the lyricism of a poetic ideal. By 1918 Modigliani, who had long been suffering from untreated tuberculosis, was gravely ill, his health destroyed by drinking and drug taking. Many of those who sat for him at this time were young, unknown and from modest origins, their faces marked by 'a hunted tenderness'. Here the delicate tracing of Baranowski's features and the long arc made by his left hand suggest the abstract refinement of a sculpture by Brancusi, while the slight inclination of the head allows the left side of the face to be broadened and flattened, emphasizing the sculptural quality of its surface. Modigliani's own experience of stone carving is strongly felt, especially in the incisive firmness of line that describes the figure's characteristic serpentine form.

Maurice de Vlaminck
La danseuse du 'Rat Mort'
1906, signed
Oil on canvas, 73 by 54 cm
(28¾ by 21¼ in)
New York $4,622,500
(£2,727,275) 13.XI.97

In 1906 André Derain rented a studio on the rue Tourlaque in Paris, and it was there that he and his friend, Maurice de Vlaminck, painted the young dancer from the 'Rat Mort' cabaret. The two paintings make a fascinating contrast, that of Vlaminck being much more unrestrained. Whilst the influence of Van Gogh is apparent, Vlaminck did not possess the keen intelligence and analytical approach of the Dutchman, and at this stage of his career saw the act of painting as an emotional release: 'What I could only have achieved in a social context by throwing a bomb – which would have led to the scaffold – I have tried to express in art, in painting, by using pure colours straight from the tube.'

Giorgio Morandi
Natura morta con pane e fruttiera
1919, signed
Oil on canvas, 45 by 59 cm
(17¾ by 23¼ in)
London £793,500
($1,317,210) 9.XII.97
From the José Luis and
Beatriz Plaza Collection

In 1918–19 Morandi produced about eight still-life paintings with enigmatic objects similar to those used by Carlo Carrà and Giorgio de Chirico, practitioners of a style of painting they had termed *Pittura Metafisica*. Items such as dressmaker mannequins, though endowed with human characteristics, acted as still-life objects and aided these artists in the creation of an eternal, passionless and unalterable quality in their

work. Deeply concerned with formal values, Morandi turned to metaphysical imagery primarily because the rounded, smooth contours of the isolated objects could supply an appealing plastic contrast to the still-life elements he explored in his art. However, unlike de Chirico and Carrà's metaphysical paintings, Morandi's aim was not to create a psychologically disturbing imagery, but to arrive at an almost

architectural compositional order. In the present work the elements are rendered as absolutes, deprived of the memory of the past and premonitions of the future. Decontextualized, they are solitary totems of a reality that has no connection with the living space outside the composition and seem to absorb light from an unknown source: cold ambers of a space devoid of any human element, beyond time.

Pierre Bonnard
La cheminée
1916, signed
Oil on canvas, 81 by 111.1 cm
(31⅞ by 43¾ in)
New York $3,632,500
(£2,215,825) 13.v.98
Property from the Margoline
Collection

Bonnard painted *La cheminée* in 1916, the year he moved to a new apartment at 56 rue Molitor, in Auteuil, which may be the setting for this daring composition. The painting reflected in the large mirror is by Maurice Denis, who had presented it to Bonnard very shortly after it was finished in 1892. Denis's figure of a reclining nude (seen in reverse in the mirror) had been conceived as decoration, and Bonnard uses the assertive flatness of

that earlier composition as a backdrop to his own more robustly formed nude. The model may have been Lucienne Dupuy de Frenelle, with whom the artist is reputed to have had a serious love affair around this time, but the posture also refers to the celebrated Antique sculpture, *The Dying Niobid*. The 1910s were a crucial period for Bonnard, marking as they do his confrontation with the legacy of the Impressionists and

what he perceived to be their 'failure to attend to form'. His response was to concentrate on composition, utilizing solid framing devices by placing his figures in spaces determined by the strict verticals and horizontals of doors, windows and, in the present example, mirrors.

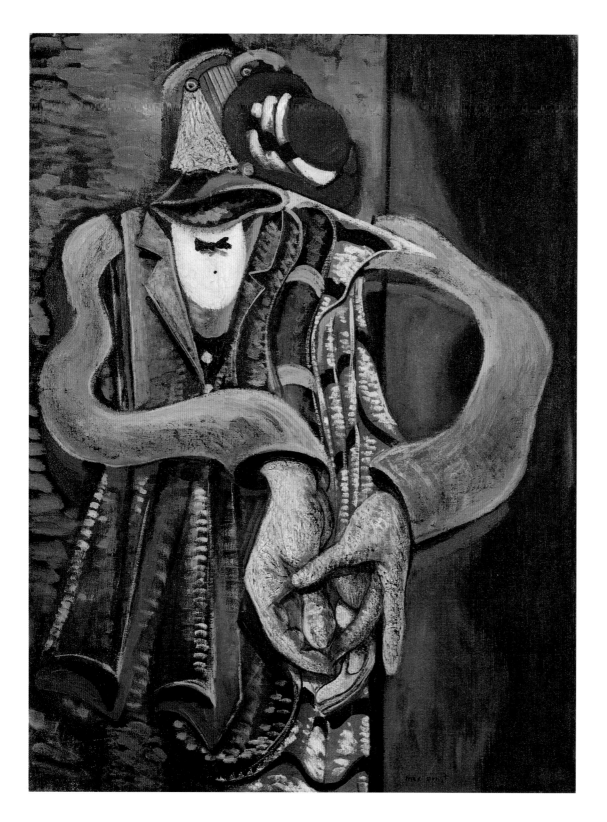

Max Ernst

Le couple ou l'accolade
1924, signed
Oil on canvas, 73 by 54 cm
(28¾ by 21¼ in)
London £694,500
($1,152,870) 8.XII.97

This pivotal work was
painted in the same year
that Surrealism was officially
declared as a movement
with the publication of
André Breton's *Manifesto of
Surrealism*. The power of the
image now mattered more
than the medium and Max
Ernst returned to oil painting
after years of experimenting
with other media, particularly
collage. Oil allowed him to
invent his motif from his
unconscious rather than
construct images from parts
culled from several sources.
Ernst produced some of his
most haunting and powerful
works during this period,
many of which have become
key emblems of
displacement and
psychological doubt in
the art of the 20th century.
In *Le couple*, the sense of
irrational and vehement
power is partly achieved
by the artist's enlargement
of the hands and by the
deliberate ambiguity he
employs by combining
two persons, a couple,
into a single figure.

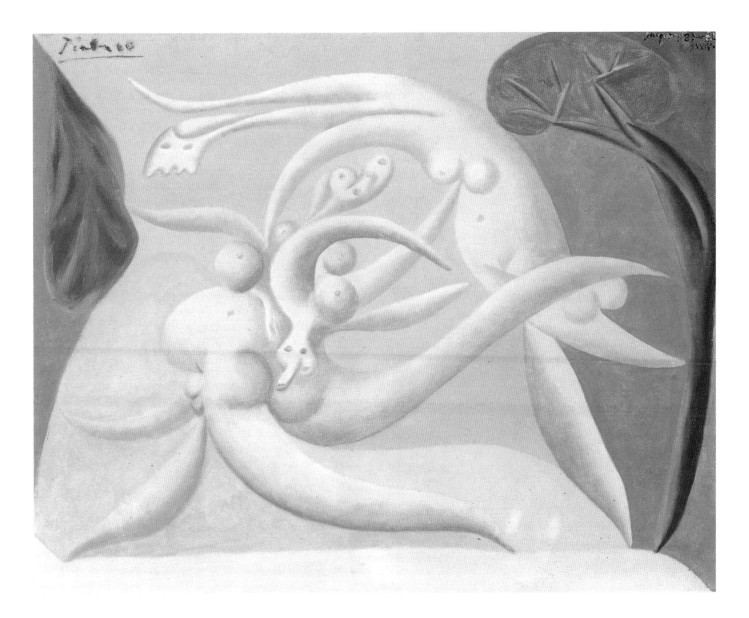

Pablo Picasso
Nus
Signed, dated and inscribed
Boisegeloup 8 Avril /XXXIV
Oil on canvas, 81.3 by 100 cm
(32 by 39⅜ in)
New York $6,052,500
(£3,570,975) 12.XI.97
From the Evelyn Sharp
Collection

This extraordinary group
of pale, boneless creatures
gambolling in a landscape
was painted during a brief
period in 1934 when Picasso
was concentrating on
depicting still lifes. The
octopus-like figures are all
formed from the same pliable
material but the profusion
and interchangeability of

body parts makes an
exact body count next to
impossible. Weightless and
seemingly innocent in their
sexual curiosity, the less than
human forms in Picasso's
phantasmagoria are among
his most remarkable
creations immediately
preceding *Guernica*.

CONTEMPORARY ART

Roy Lichtenstein
The Ring
Signed and dated '62 on
the reverse
Oil on canvas, 121.9 by
177.8 cm (48 by 70 in)
New York $2,202,500
(£1,299,475) 19.XI.97

The Ring is a prized example
of Lichtenstein's early comic
strip paintings, a series that
has been identified as the
artist's 'mock-heroic
adventures for grown-ups'.
Painted to resemble a single
frame from a cartoon strip,
this work depicts a romantic
encounter between a man

and woman. It generates
excitement by anticipating
the couple's engagement
without conclusively
depicting it. Will the action
be consummated and what
will the next frame in the
story reveal? By engaging
the viewer in suspense,
Lichtenstein manipulates

the depth of our involvement
in the narrative, using the
cartoon technique to remind
us of its essentially fictitious
nature.

Mark Rothko
No. 14, 1960
Signed and dated *1960* on
the reverse
Oil on canvas, 290.8 by
268.6 cm (114½ by 105⅝ in)
New York $5,942,500
(£3,506,075) 19.XI.97

Rothko's passion as an artist
was to explore the
intellectual and abstract
potentials of painting; *No. 14,
1960* poetically achieves his
intention to create a spiritual
art. In mature works such as
this, pure colour and a sense
of light became Rothko's
vocabulary for expressing his
inner perceptions and
engaging the viewer's
unconscious responses.
Rothko wanted his larger
paintings, as well as room
installations of a group of
paintings, to envelop and
overwhelm the viewer,
allowing the sensuous and
spiritual presence of colour
to act as a doorway into
another transcendent reality.
As he stated in a 1957
interview, colour expresses
'basic human emotions –
tragedy, ecstasy, doom... The
people who weep before my
pictures are having the same
religious experience I had
when I painted them'.

Bruce Nauman
Good Boy/Bad Boy
1986–87
Neon and glass tubing mounted on metal monolith, 349.3 by 548.6 by 37.5 cm (137½ by 216 by 14¾ in)
New York $2,202,500 (£1,299,475) 19.XI.97
Property from the Collection of Camille and Paul Oliver-Hoffmann

Good Boy/Bad Boy is the culmination of Bruce Nauman's exploration of visual and verbal puns in the form of large-scale neon installations. Well-versed in the writings of Ludwig Wittgenstein, Alain Robbe-Grillet and Samuel Beckett, Nauman set out to explore how entire phrases can be turned inside-out and then reconstituted to serve his purposes. Exploring the value systems of 'good' and 'evil' and how they relate to the human condition, he stages an installation of powerful statements. On entering the darkened space, the viewer is immediately surprised by the first flash of colour. With each new hue comes another statement, enticing the viewer to continue watching and reading, provoked perhaps by statements about 'you' and 'I' and 'us'.

OPPOSITE

Jean-Michel Basquiat
Red Savoy
Signed, titled and dated
Nov. 83
Acrylic and oilstick on canvas, 168 by 152 cm (66 by 59¾ in)
London £353,500 ($583,575) 10.XII.97

Red Savoy is an energetic and powerful crystallization of all the cultural tributaries that fed into Basquiat's pool of motifs and defining techniques as an artist. It is one of a series of eight works from 1983 in this format and style, when the artist was at the pinnacle of his creative powers. It is uncompromisingly urban in flavour, with references to graffiti art combined with a list of such phrases as 'Another Hair Do', 'Blue Bird' and 'Parker's Mood'. This latter reference to the legendary trumpeter Charlie Parker sets the tone and key to the jazzy interpretation of the Black hero figure, which features with fists raised in victory and defiance, either musician, boxer or track star, in so many of Basquiat's works. The score at the top of the canvas is a quotation from a Parker piece and sets the canvas ringing with vibrant harmony. The approximate handling of the figure in a neo-expressionist manner, while alluding to primitive art, is a wonderful example of Basquiat's intuitive, imaginative style.

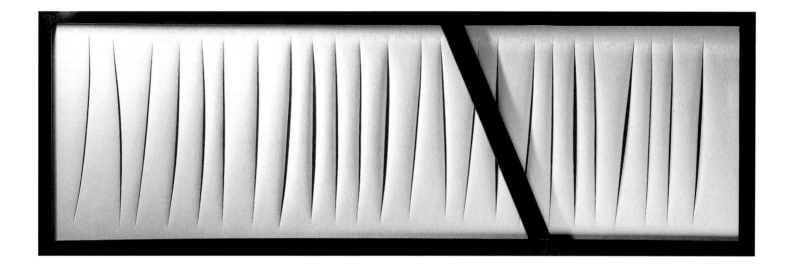

Lucio Fontana
Concetto Spaziale, Attese
1965, signed, titled and
inscribed *ieri è venuta a
trovarmi Tro-tro Klein*
Waterpaint on canvas
with lacquered wood, 70 by
200 cm (27½ by 78¾ in)
London £529,500 ($878,970)
2.VII.98
From the Collection of Carla
Panicali, Rome

In 1965, the year in which this
work was executed, Fontana
wrote, 'I do not want to make
a painting: I want to open up
space ... I make a hole in the
canvas and the infinite
comes through.' Here, on a
pure white canvas, 24 vertical
slashes create a masterpiece
of rare lyricism and poetic
symphony. The black frame
operates as a visual divide,

creating two asymmetric
sections. It is, as Fred Licht
has described, 'a signal
which challenges our
understanding in the context
of the softer, somewhat
random slashes behind it.'
This work set a new world
auction record for a Fontana
slash painting.

Alexander Calder
Brontosaurus
Signed with initials and
dated 70
Painted metal stabile, overall
213.4 by 152.4 by 365.8 cm
(84 by 60 by 144 in)
New York $860,500
(£507,695) 19.XI.97

As early as his first
monumental 'stabile', *Whale*,
in 1937, Calder created forms
that relate to animal shapes,
especially those that are the
most fluid and noble. The
term 'stabile', coined by
Marcel Duchamp and Jean
Arp in 1932, implies a sense

of static weight, in contrast
to the lightness and
movement suggested in
'mobile'. However, Calder
purposely chose forms that
allowed his sculptures to
'appear to rest as lightly as
possible on the ground, to
appear to rise from the

ground or to be capable of
instantaneous movement'.
Both the whale and the
dinosaur are creatures
of sinuous line, large
proportion and slow,
rhythmic movement.
Brontosaurus embodies
these characteristics in the

graceful sweep of the 'tail'
and the simplified curved
shapes of the 'torso' that
touch the earth lightly at
only three points.

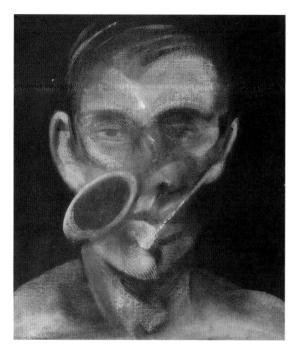 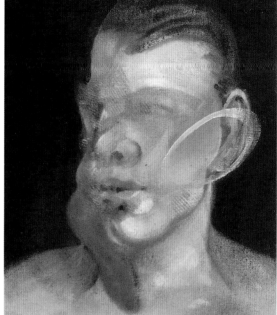

Gerhard Richter
Seestück (See-See)
Signed and dated 1970
Oil on canvas, 200 by
200 cm (78¾ by 78¾ in)
London £1,431,500
($2,376,290) 2.VII.98

Gerhard Richter's series of
seascapes, executed between
1969 and 1970, display
glorious and striking
differences in colour and
atmosphere. Amongst these
works *Seapiece (Sea-Sea)*
evokes a mystical mood in
its subtle tonal variations,
becoming a paragon of calm
and serenity. However, upon
lengthy contemplation, the
viewer realizes that the
seascape is as artificial as the
paint with which it is created,
for, as its title suggests, this
work differs crucially from all
but one other in the series in
that the horizon represents a
border between two different
seas, not the sea and sky. In
subverting the tradition of
the seascape in art history
this painting becomes a
question not only of
representation, but also of
manipulation. It connects
firmly with the intellectual
agenda of the artist's earlier
photo-paintings, engaging as
it does with issues of reality
and irreality, and the rigours
of mimesis. *Seapiece (Sea-
Sea)* mesmerizes through
Richter's unparalleled ability
to fuse the polarities of
beauty and irony, of
invention and appropriation
within a single canvas.

Francis Bacon
Studies for Portrait – Diptych
Each: signed, titled and
dated 1976
Each: oil on canvas, 35 by
30 cm (13¾ by 11⅞ in)
London £408,500 ($678,110)
2.VII.98

Between 1975 and 1976
Bacon painted 14 portraits of
the distinguished American
wildlife photographer and
author, Peter Beard, of which
this diptych is one. Beard got
to know Bacon in London in
the mid 1960s and spent a
great deal of time
accompanying the artist
around the bars, restaurants
and clubs he frequented at
night. Beard was strikingly
good-looking and it is
certainly the case that these
portraits show a likeness to
the sitter that is less altered
and obscured by distortion
than many of the other

paintings Bacon made of
his friends. Nonetheless,
Bacon's habit of making
non-rational marks to convey
what he called 'the mystery
of fact' is also in evidence,
notably in the dark ellipse
in the left-hand panel,
which Michel Leiris once
defined as the 'heightening
accents' in this artist's work.
It is tempting to read such
shapes as identifiable
objects, but as Leiris has
suggested, these exist
purely as 'capricious or
disorderly elements
(expressive of liberties
taken or rules broken)'.

PRINTS

Albrecht Dürer
Coat-of-arms with a Skull
Engraving, 1503
22.4 by 15.8 cm (8¾ by
6¼ in)
London £102,700
($171,509) 30.VI.98

Engraved in 1503, when
Dürer was 32, this highly
wrought and brilliantly
executed print was a
demonstration of the
maturity and completeness
of his technique, able equally
to define glittering metal, or
the softness of hair and
feathers, whilst the fluttering

ornament almost relegates
his predecessor, Martin
Schongauer, to the Middle
Ages. The proximity of death
and life had long been a
popular subject for German
and Northern artists, and
here perhaps reflects
knowledge of the drypoints of
the Master of the Housebook.

László Moholy-Nagy
Konstruktion
(Kestnermappe 6)
Portfolio comprising the set
of six lithographs, two
printed in colour, four
printed in black and greys,
1922–23, each signed in
pencil, with justification, this
copy numbered 43, from the
edition of 50, published by
Ludwig Ey and Eckart von
Sidow, Hanover
Each sheet 60 by 44 cm
(23⅝ by 17¼ in)
London £91,700 ($152,222)
9.XII.97

The art institute Kestner-
Gesellschaft was founded in
1916 by the citizens of the
city of Hanover to promote
an understanding of the
contemporary arts. In 1923
the institute organized the
publication of a series of six
portfolios, each containing
six lithographs, to which
Moholy-Nagy contributed
the sixth portfolio. In this
medium the young artist was
able to refine differences of
tonality and create an
awkward balance of dark and
light strips that was to endow
the Kestner lithographs with
a sense of monumentality.
It was also in this year that
Walter Gropius invited
Moholy-Nagy to join the
Weimar Bauhaus, thus
heralding a move away
from spiritual conceptions
of art at the school towards
the art of industrial
production and the machine.

Henri de Toulouse-Lautrec
Elles
Suite of 10 lithographs, 9
printed in colours, signed in
pencil, 1896, each numbered
in ink *Serie 29*, from the
edition of 100, published by
Gustave Pellet, Paris
Each sheet approximately 52
by 40 cm (20½ by 15¾ in)
New York $767,000
(£452,530) 8.XI.97

This rare set of lithographs is
the artist's definitive work
from the period and
represents one of the
pinnacles of colour
lithography. Lautrec regarded
this medium as a primary
means of artistic expression,
and one that afforded him
great flexibility. Between 1892
and 1895, Lautrec was a
regular visitor to the brothels
of rue des Moulins, rue
d'Ambroise and rue Joubert,
observing, sketching and
often living with the
prostitutes, seeking to
portray them without the
morality or overt eroticism
common in other artists'
depictions. In these
examples, Lautrec combines
a powerful line and broad
planes of colour with original
designs and a mastery of
technique.

**Francisco José de Goya y
Lucientes**
*El Famoso Americano,
Mariano Ceballos*
Lithograph from the *Bulls of
Bordeaux*, 1825, from the
edition of 100, published by
Gaulon, Bordeaux
Sheet: 43 by 58.5 cm
(16⅞ by 23 in)
New York $79,500 (£47,700)
1.V.98
Property from the
Metropolitan Museum of Art

Goya made his first
lithographs at the age of 73
and within six years had
become a master of the
medium, approaching it with
the same ease of expression
as he achieved with paint on
canvas. Here the main
figures are drawn in a dark
rich crayon, with the
highlights scraped away, like
the flickering rope across the
bull's back. The spectators in
the background are
suggested in a calligraphic
short hand, drawn together
and animated with scraped
highlights.

Andy Warhol

Myths: Mickey Mouse
Screenprint printed in
colours with diamond dust,
1981, signed in pencil,
numbered 50/200,
published by Ronald
Feldman Fine Arts, Inc.,
New York
Sheet: 96.5 by 96.5 cm
(38 by 38 in)
London £24,150 ($40,089)
12.XII.97

Warhol's art is characterized
by the single, iconic image,
such as a soup can, Coca-
cola bottle, Mickey Mouse or
Marilyn Monroe. Isolated,
decontextualized and often
repeated, these works stand
as ambivalent symbols of
the 20th century.

Claes Oldenburg

*Double Screwarch Bridge
(State III)*
Etching, aquatint and
monotype printed in colours,
1981, signed in pencil, dated
and inscribed *A. P. VI/XIII*,
one of 13 artist's proofs,
aside from the numbered
edition of 25, published by
Multiples, Inc., New York
Sheet: 59.4 by 128.5 cm
(23⅜ by 50⅝ in)
New York $34,500 (£20,700)
2.V.98

Published during 1980–81,
the three states of *Double
Screwarch Bridge* represent
a defining moment in Claes
Oldenburg's print oeuvre.
Employing the same copper
plates used in *State II*,
Oldenburg printed *State III*,
the final and most complex
version, in colour and further
added washes of ink directly
to the plate so that every
print is a unique monotype.
Monumental in subject
matter and technique, this
print unifies many of
Oldenburg's ideas as a
printmaker and draughtsman.

PHOTOGRAPHS

McDonell & Co., Buffalo
Indian Chief – Upper Canada
1850–51
Half-plate daguerreotype,
hand-tinted, in plush lined,
embossed leather case
London £45,500 ($75,530)
7.v.98
From the Collections of the
8th and 9th Earls of Elgin

This portrait of a Canadian
Indian chief posing proudly
in plumed headdress is
perhaps the single most
remarkable portrait to be
brought back from his travels
by the 8th Earl of Elgin. Lord
Elgin made an important
contribution to British and
Empire history in his various
roles, first as Governor
General of Canada,
subsequently as emissary to
Japan and China and finally
as Governor General and
Viceroy of India. It has been
suggested that the subject
of this daguerreotype may
be Maungwudaus, a
Mississauga Indian, born
in 1811 on the Credit River
reserve just west of present-
day Toronto.

EW 9/50

Edward Weston
Mexico 1924

Edward Weston
Circus Tent
Signed and dated 1924
Platinum-palladium print,
no. 9 of a proposed edition
of 50, 23.8 by 18.1 cm (9⅜ by
7⅛ in)
New York $266,500
(£159,900) 7.IV.98

After attending a
performance of the Russian
Circus in Mexico City in 1924,
Weston and his lover Tina
Modotti returned to the site
the next day with their
cameras. Weston turned his
Graflex toward the folds,
poles and ropes of the circus
tent, producing this striking
image, one of his earliest and
most significant forays into
pure abstraction. In a 1924
exhibition of Weston's work,
painter Diego Rivera chose
Circus Tent as his favourite,
stating that he would 'rather
have a good photograph
than a realistic painting'. The
price for this photograph
represents a world record for
the artist.

LITERARY PROPERTY

GEMINI

CANCER

CANIS
MINOR

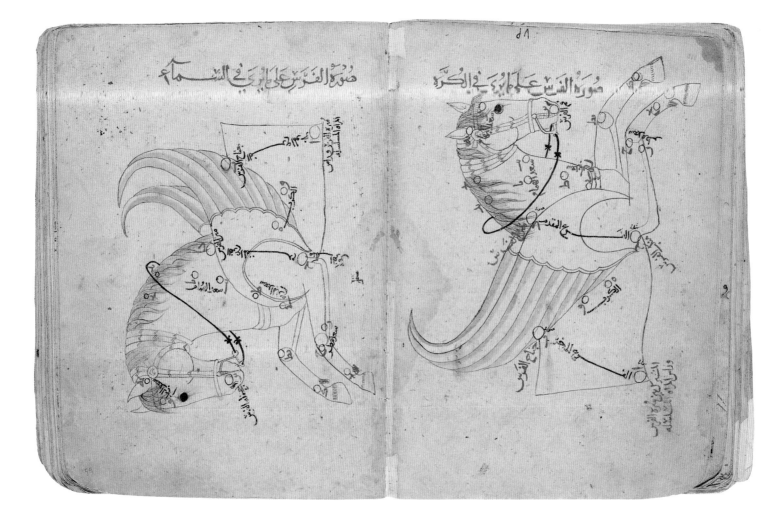

The *Kitab Suwar al-Kawakib (The Book of Fixed Stars)* of Abu'l-Husain Abd al-Rahman ibn Umar ibn Muhammad al-Sufi
Copied and illustrated by Ali ibn Abd al-Jalil ibn Ali ibn Muhammad, Baghdad, dated Muharram–Safar AH 519/February–March AD 1125 Illustrated Arabic manuscript on paper, 180 leaves and 62 original line drawings, 23.7 by 17.1 cm (9⅜ by 6¾ in) London £969,500 ($1,619,065) 29.IV.98

Al-Sufi was one of the great medieval Arab astronomers. He was tutor to the Buyid Sultan Adud al-Dawla, for whom this text was written in AD 965, and, briefly, Astronomer Royal. The *Kitab Suwar al-Kawakib* is based on the work of Ptolemy and early Arab astronomers, as well as the traditions of the Bedouin tribes, and presents lists of stellar co-ordinates and their relations to the zodiac. This previously unrecorded copy is immensely important for

the history of Islamic science and painting. Not only is it the third earliest extant copy, it is among the half-dozen earliest illustrated Islamic manuscripts of any text. The drawings, with their mixture of Hellenistic, Arab and oriental characteristics, are individually significant for showing details of 12th-century accoutrements. The manuscript is also unusual for containing a colophon giving not only the date of copying and the name of the

scribe, but also details of the manuscripts the scribe used as models, by whom those manuscripts were copied and to whom they belonged. This wealth of information offers scholars a fascinating insight into the patronage and production of such a work. The price achieved for the *Kitab Suwar-al Kawakib* set a world auction record for any oriental manuscript.

**Vinod Putra of Hindol:
a Prince with a Maiden
on each Arm**
Bahu (Jammu), c. 1700–10,
21 by 21 cm (8¼ by 8¼ in)
New York, $60,250 (£36,150)
26.111.98

This intimate scene in a
small pavilion features a
prince resting against an
orange bolster with a richly
jewelled woman on either
side. The differences in scale
between the figures serve to

emphasize their relative
importance. Many paintings
from this series were brought
to the West in about 1920 by
Ananda K. Coomaraswamy.
Today, over half can be
accounted for, with 32 in the

Victoria and Albert Museum
in London and six in the
Museum of Fine Arts,
Boston.

WESTERN MANUSCRIPTS

The Burdett Psalter and Hours
Made for an official of the Knights Hospitaller, probably for Jean de Villiers, Grand Master of the Order, illuminated by the Méliacin Master
Paris, c. 1282–86
Manuscript on vellum, 106 leaves, 23.3 by 15.4 cm (9⅛ by 6⅛ in)
London £2,751,500 ($4,595,005) 23.VI.98

The dazzling appearance on the market of this extraordinary manuscript was one of the great surprises of 1998. The manuscript is a work of the highest quality, illustrated with 26 paintings by the leading Parisian illuminator of the late 13th century, known as the Méliacin Master. It was commissioned probably by Jean de Villiers, French Grand Prior then Grand Master of the Order, who witnessed the fall of the Holy Land to the Muslims at Acre in 1291. The manuscript was in East Anglia by around 1300. From 1634 to 1990 it descended through the Burdett family, being finely bound in around 1720. Until 1998 it was entirely unrecorded and unpublished.

King Arthur and Queen Guinivere attending the Christmas joust at Camelot
One of a group of seven miniatures cut from an illuminated manuscript of *Le Livre de Lancelot del Lac*
Paris, *c.* 1444
London £89,500 ($151,255)
2.XII.97
From the Collection of the late Neil F. Phillips, QC

These miniatures are securely attributable to the Dunois Master, an illuminator who takes his name from the Hours of Jean d'Orléans, comte de Dunois. There is evidence for identifying him with Jean Haincelin, an artist documented as working for the duc d'Orléans, the comte's brother. In 1444 Haincelin sold a *Lancelot*, probably the present example, to Prigent de Coëtivy, who was Admiral of France and married to the daughter of the legendary murderer 'Bluebeard'. The manuscript was apparently cut up by the 16th century. The present miniatures later belonged to Joachim Napoléon, fifth Prince Murat (1856–1932).

Bartholomaeus Anglicus
Le Livre de la Propriété des Choses
In the French translation of Jean Corbechon
Paris, *c.* 1400
Illuminated manuscript on vellum, 328 leaves, 40.8 by 30.5 cm (16 by 12 in)
London £463,500 ($774,045)
23.VI.98

This vast manuscript was made for a courtier of Philippe le Hardi (d.1404), Duke of Burgundy and brother of the king of France. It has 61 miniatures, which are attributable to the Parisian illuminator Jean de Nizières. The text is one of the great secular encyclopedias of the late Middle Ages, on cosmography, science, medicine, natural history, and so forth. The present manuscript was last sold at Sotheby's in Lord Ashburnham's sale in 1901 for £295.

MUSIC MANUSCRIPTS

Johannes Brahms
Autograph manuscripts
of the two Clarinet Sonatas,
Op. 120
Signed, dated and inscribed
by the composer to the
dedicatee, the clarinettist
Richard Mühlfeld, 67 pages,
oblong folio, Ischl, 1894
London £441,500 ($741,720)
5.XII.97

These manuscripts achieved
the highest price of any late
Romantic music manuscripts
at auction. They caused
considerable excitement
among musicians and
scholars as they were
Brahms's actual composition
manuscripts: the composer
habitually destroyed any such
manuscripts that contained

the early stages of
composition. Here the
opening of the last
movement of the second
sonata is shown, containing
early drafts of the theme that
forms the basis of the
movement as a whole.
Instead of writing out a fair
copy and destroying the
original, Brahms presented it

to Richard Mühlfeld, the
instrumentalist whose
playing inspired this and
other celebrated clarinet
works of the composer's
final golden period. The
manuscripts remained
unknown to scholars for
almost a century and were
finally consigned for sale by
Mühlfeld's descendants.

Felix Mendelssohn
View of Leipzig in Winter
Inscribed and dedicated to
the composer William
Sterndale Bennett, Leipzig,
1839
Coloured washes on paper,
overall size 21.2 by 21.9 cm
(8½ by 8⅝ in)
London £79,600 ($128,952)
21.v.98

This previously unknown
watercolour by
Mendelssohn, apparently
painted from the window of
his lodgings in Leipzig,
shows the Thomasschule
where Johann Sebastian
Bach worked and where he
composed the *St Matthew
Passion*. Mendelssohn
himself conducted the first
performance of the work in
modern times, and was
instrumental in the revival
of Bach's music in general.

The 'Novello Organ Book'
c. 1650s
329 pages, folio
London £89,500 ($144,990)
21.v.98

An important source of 17th-
century Roman Catholic
organ music, this Anglo-
Flemish manuscript contains
over 100 compositions,
including music by
Sweelinck, Kerckhoven and
others, mainly written by
English hands of the 1650s.
The manuscript is inscribed
on the covers by the
composer and musical
antiquary Vincent Novello,
who donated it to the Musical
Antiquarian Society in 1844.

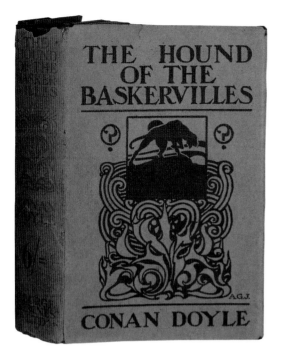

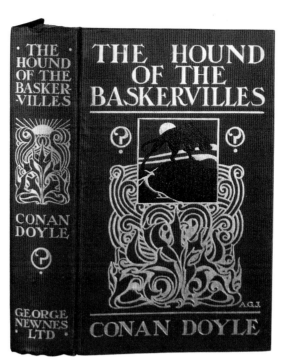

Sir Arthur Conan Doyle
The Hound of the Baskervilles
First edition, with original
dust-jacket, frontispiece and
16 illustrations by Sidney
Paget, George Newnes Ltd,
1902
London £80,700 ($132,348)
16.VII.98

Copies of the first edition of
this famous novel in its
original dust-jacket are
extremely rare. Only two
others are recorded, one in
the Bodleian Library and
another in Texas, and none
has previously been sold at
auction. The novel was
inspired by a legend
mentioned by Doyle's friend
Bertram Fletcher Robinson
during a golfing holiday in
1901. This was probably the
tale of the Black Hound of
Hergest, associated with
the Vaughan family of
Herefordshire, which Doyle
transferred to Dartmoor. He
researched the area with
Robinson, commenting in a
letter to his mother, 'we are
going to do a small book
together "The Hound of the
Baskervilles" – a real
creeper... Holmes is at his
very best, and it is a highly
dramatic idea'.

Girard Thibault
Académie de l'espée
Engraved title by A. Bolsvert,
portrait of Thibault, nine
leaves of coats-of-arms, 46
plates by Crispin de Pas,
Latsman, Stockins,
Sherwonters, Bloswer and
others
First edition, [Leiden], 1628
London £31,050 ($50,922)
5.VI.98

A copy of this book in the
library at Versailles contains
an additional leaf,
Avertissement au lecteur,
announcing the late
publication of this work due
to the death of the author and
signed from the Elzevir Press
at Leiden, August, 1630.

Ptolemy

Cosmographia
Translated by Jacobus
Angelus, cartography by
Dom Nicolaus Germanus,
Ulm: Lienhart Holl, 16 July
1482, Super-Royal folio
New York $1,267,500
(£760,500) 26.VI.98

This book was one of the
finest and most ambitious
printing projects of the 15th
century, and the first atlas to
be printed outside Italy. It
was also the first complete
printed version of the
Ptolemaic atlas as revised
and supplemented by the
Renaissance cartographer
Dom Nicolaus Germanus. A
Benedictine from the diocese
of Breslau (*c.* 1420–*c.*1490),
Dom Nicolaus prepared a
series of magnificent vellum
manuscript atlases for
presentation to Italian
dignitaries while he was
based in Florence. This
edition incorporated the
27 maps based directly on
Ptolemy's second-century AD
descriptions, along with five
modern maps constructed
by Dom Nicolaus – Spain,
Italy, France, Palestine and
northern Europe, including
Iceland and Greenland.

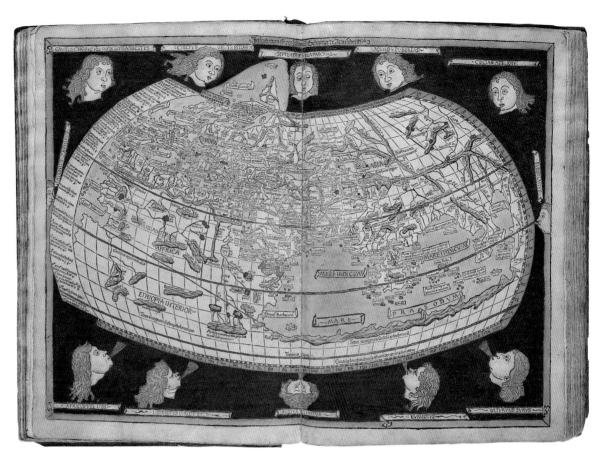

Johann Elert Bode

*Uranographia, sive Astrorum
descriptio*
20 large engraved celestial
charts, Berlin, 1801
London £27,600 ($46,368)
4.XII.97

Astronomer Royal Johann
Elert Bode was one of
Germany's most influential
astronomers. His celebrated
celestial atlas, the
Uranographia, was the last
and most comprehensive
of its type. This fine copy
was sold with Bode's star
catalogue, *Allegemeine
Beschreibung und
Nachweisung der Gestirne*,
1801, which was intended
to accompany the
Uranographia. The two works
are rarely found together.

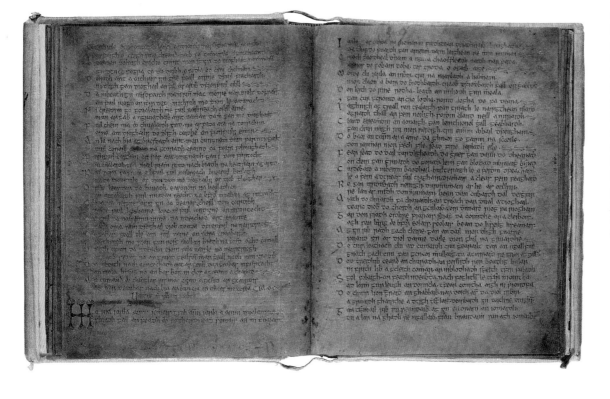

**The archive of Edith Hahn:
German passport as Edith
Sara Hahn, stamped with
a J, 1939**
The archive: over 800 pages,
1918–18, the letters 1941–44
London £100,500
($168,840) 5.XII.97

Edith Hahn was a Jewish law
student in Vienna at the time
of the *Anschluss* in 1938,
when she was forced to
abandon her studies. In 1941
she was sent to labour
camps in Germany but
returned to Vienna in 1942
where she adopted a false
identity using papers
provided by a friend. Edith
moved to Munich and
worked as a Red Cross
nursing auxiliary, a
profession strictly reserved
for Aryans, and met and
married a German divorcee.
The archive contains papers
relating to this period of
Edith's life and is one of the
most extensive collections of
such documents to survive.
It includes letters to and
from her fiancé Dr Joseph
Rosenfeld, written while
Edith was in the Osterburg
and Aschersleben labour
camps; photographs,
including illicit images of
labour camps, and identity
papers showing Edith as a
Jewish resident of Vienna
and her false identity as a
German.

**The Nugent Manuscript of
Irish Bardic Poetry**
An Elizabethan 'duanaire'
containing nearly 50 poems
in Gaelic dating from the
13th to the 15th centuries,
49 leaves, quarto
London £155,500 ($256,575)
11.XII.97

It is highly unlikely that an
Irish manuscript of this date
and calibre will ever appear
at auction again. None has
been sold since the Book of
Armagh was offered for sale
in 1831. As an example of
medieval Irish book
production this codex
represents the last link in a
chain of book production
that stretches back to at least
the seventh century, and a
history of graphic design that
is possibly the oldest in the
world. This collection of
poetry, originally composed
for the most part for
recitation, was made during
the Elizabethan era and
comprises miscellaneous
poems dating from each of
the previous four centuries.
It was apparently compiled
for the Nugent family of
Westmeath, in whose
possession it remained
for 400 years.

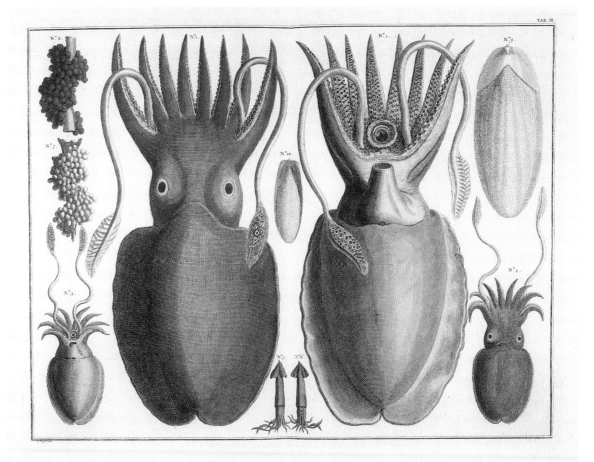

Albertus Seba

Locupletissimi rerum naturalium thesauri accurata descriptio
4 volumes in 8, first edition, Amsterdam, 1734–65
London £331,500 ($556,920)
4.XII.97

This sumptuous catalogue is a record of the second and largest cabinet of natural rarities formed by Albertus Seba, a German-born apothecary who became rich in the service of the Dutch East India Company. It includes mammals, birds, plants, insects, butterflies, reptiles, fish, crustaceans, shells, minerals and fossils. Seba's first collection was sold in 1717 to Peter the Great of Russia for a vast sum. However, his new cabinet soon surpassed the first and was admired by Linnaeus, although he denounced Seba's seven-headed Hydra as a fake. The binding for this catalogue is by the great Viennese master, Georg Friedrich Krauss, and is one of a number executed for Duke Albert of Saxe-Teschen, a celebrated collector of his time.

Muhammed Sadiq Bey

A complete set of albumen prints of Mecca and Medina 1880–81, comprising 18 photographs, presented as 13 images
London £1,376,500 ($2,257,460) 4.VI.98

Sadiq Bey was a pioneer in the history of Arabian photography and exploration. He was both the first to photograph the Holy Cities of Mecca and Medina and the first to produce detailed surveys of the area north of Medina. Bey's photographs were widely celebrated in their day, winning him the Gold Medal at the Venice *Exposition Géographique* in 1881. He was also honoured at the Philadelphia anniversary exhibition of 1876.

Beatrix Potter
Signed autograph letter in which Beatrix Potter relates the story of 'a frog named Jeremy Fisher'
Illustrated with 7 ink drawings, octavo, 6 pages
London £144,500 ($239,870)
7.v.98

Mr Jeremy Fisher was Beatrix Potter's first published imaginative character and this picture letter marks his first appearance. It was written on 5th September 1893 and was sent to Eric Moore, the second son of Potter's old governess, Annie. The letter was last seen in public when it was sold at Sotheby's on 25th March 1947. Its reappearance at auction in May achieved a new world record, making it the most expensive Beatrix Potter item ever sold.

Hans Christian Andersen
Picture book compiled by Andersen for his god-daughter Rigmor Stampe
Approximately 300 pages of paper-cuttings, engravings, illustrations and manuscript notes or verses by Hans Andersen, quarto, 1852
London £353,500 ($590,345)
31.x.97

Andersen is known to have made about a dozen such albums for the children of his friends, including various members of the Collin family. Rigmor Stampe, for whom this book was produced, was the daughter of Edvard Collin, a close childhood friend of Andersen's. Rigmor's mother Jonna

described in a letter to Andersen in 1853 how the little girl had come running up to her 'dragging her big picture book' to tell her how much she loved the pictures in it, 'It's Anser [her name for Andersen], Mama, he cut out all the ladies'. The other albums are in institutional collections.

The Holy Bible, containing the Old Testament and the New
Translated by John Eliot into the American Indian language, Natick dialect; Cambridge, Massachusetts: Samuel Green and Marmaduke Johnson, 1661–63, 2 parts in one volume, quarto
New York $244,500
(£144,255) 25.XI.97

A first edition of the first Bible to be printed in America, this was intended for distribution in England by Eliot's sponsor, the Corporation for the Propagation of the Gospel among Indians in New England. Eliot's remarkable translation is also the first time that the Bible was printed in a new language specifically for evangelization.

A new type font was created to accommodate the Natick language that included extra sorts of the letters *k* and *q* and one special character.

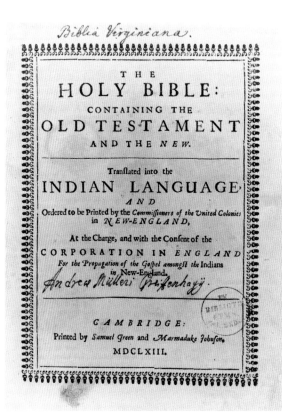

Prince Maximilian Alexander Philipp zu Wied-Neuwied
Reise in das innere Nord-America in den Jahren 1832 bis 1834
Coblenz: J. Hoelscher, 1839–41
New York $255,500
(£155,855) 16.1.98
From the Stanley Paul Sax Collection

Prince Maximilian engaged Karl Bodmer to record his travels among the American Plains Indians from 1832 to 1834, during a time when the Plains and the Rockies were virtually unknown. This book became one of the most celebrated texts on American Indian life and the American frontier. The royal ethnologist and his artist encountered many Indian peoples, including the Mandans and Blackfeet, as they journeyed up the Missouri River. The plates made from Bodmer's sketches were the first truly accurate depictions of the Plains Indians to reach the general public. The 1837 smallpox epidemic killed more than half the Blackfeet and almost all the Mandans, making this account the primary source of information on those lost cultures.

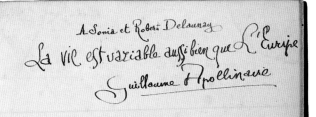

LE BESTIAIRE

OU

CORTÈGE D'ORPHÉE.

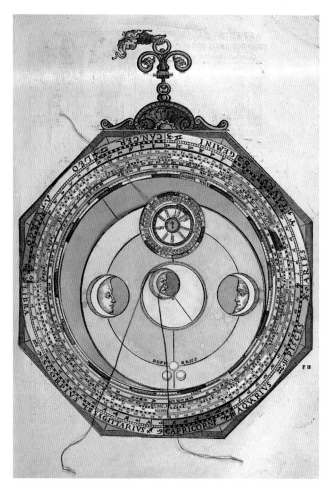

Guillaume Apollinaire, illustrated by Raoul Dufy
Le Bestiare; ou cortège d'Orphée
Paris: Deplanche, 1911
New York $244,500
(£146,700) 21.IV.98
From the Jaime Ortiz-Patiño Collection

This presentation copy of one of the first French illustrated books of the 20th century is a highly important association copy uniting four major figures of L'École de Paris. Inscribed by Apollinaire to Robert and Sonia Delaunay, the book has a magnificent painted binding by Sonia Delaunay, one of only three painted bindings believed to have been executed by her. The vivid 'simultaneous' paintings done directly on to the surface of a quite ordinary morocco binding clearly anticipate in composition, colour, format and quality the astounding designs she would later produce.

Petrus Apianus
Astronomicum Caesareum
Ingolstadt: at the author's press, May 1540, Imperial folio
New York $442,500
(£265,500) 21.IV.98
From the Jaime Ortiz-Patiño Collection

Previously owned by Harrison D. Horblit, this copy is a magnificent example of 16th-century bookmaking. The *Astronomicum Caesareum* contains a broad analysis of Ptolemaic astronomy and is notable for Apianus's pioneering observations on comets, particularly his discovery that comets always point their tails away from the sun. The elaborate folio includes more than 100 woodcut and typographic diagrams, vignettes and illustrations in the text, many with movable parts.

Alexandre Dumas
Les trois mousquetaires
Paris: Baudry, 1844,
8 volumes, octavo
New York $90,500 (£54,300)
21.IV.98
From the Jaime Ortiz-Patiño
Collection

Bound in half-green morocco gilt over blind-diapered green boards, this remarkably fresh first edition of Dumas's swashbuckling adventure extends to eight volumes. It was originally owned by the comte de Dietrichstein, whose signature appears on the verso of each front free endpaper.

Danse macabre
Ed. Pierre Desrey, Paris: Guy Marchant for Geoffroy de Marnef, (Friday) 15th October 1490, Chancery folio
New York $321,500 (£192,900) 21.IV.98
From the Jaime Ortiz-Patiño Collection

The first Latin edition of one of the finest French woodcuts of the 15th century, the Paris *Danse macabre* established an iconography that has been immensely popular over 500 years of book illustration and printmaking. The frieze-like woodcuts show successive pairs of figures, one secular and one religious, being 'danced to death' by a skeleton. Their ultimate source was the Dance of Death mural paintings of 1425, long since lost, in the gallery of the Franciscan cemetery of the Holy Innocents in Paris. The original owner of this copy, Michael Hummelberger of Ravensburg, was a German student in Paris who was a friend of the humanists Lefèvre d'Étaples, Beatus Rhenanus and Hieronymus Münzer.

WE, JOHN ADAMS, BENJAMIN FRANKLIN AND JOHN JAY, THREE OF THE MINISTERS PLENIPOTENTIARY OF THE UNITED STATES OF AMERICA, for making Peace with Great Britain, TO ALL Captains or Commanders of ships of War privateers or armed Vessels belonging to the said States or to either of them, or to any of the Citizens of the same AND TO ALL others whom these Presents may concern, SEND GREETING.

WHEREAS Peace and Amity is agreed upon between the said United States and his Britannic Majesty, and a suspension of Hostilities to take Place at different Periods in different Places hath also been agreed upon by their respective Plenipotentiaries. AND WHEREAS it hath been further agreed by the said Plenipotentiaries, to exchange Passports for merchant Vessels, to the end that such as shall be provided with them, shall be exempted from Capture altho' found in Latitudes at a time prior to the taking Place of the said suspension of Hostilities therein. NOW THEREFORE KNOW YE that free Passport, Licence and Permission is hereby given to the *Eagle, Burthen* 230 *Tons, John Sanders* commander now lying at the Port of *London* and bound from thence to *Jamaica* AND WE do earnestly enjoin upon and recommend to you to let and suffer the said Vessel to pass unmolested to her destined Port, and if need be, to afford her all such succour and Aid as Circumstances and Humanity may require.

GIVEN under our Hands and Seals at Paris on the *Sixth* Day of *february* in the year of Our Lord 1783.

John Adams.

B Franklin

John Jay

John Adams, Benjamin Franklin and John Jay
Broadside Proclamation of Peace Addressed to Commanders of Ships of War
Paris, 6th February 1783, 34.6 by 22.9 cm (13⅝ by 9 in)
New York $74,000 (£44,400)
26.VI.98

This very rare proclamation is signed by three American peace commissioners and was printed for them in Paris by P. D. Pierres. The broadside document served as a passport allowing the English vessel *Eagle*, commanded by John Sanders, to sail unmolested from the port of London to Jamaica. The passport was issued just two days after the British proclaimed the official cessation of hostilities between Britain and the former American colonies. This is the first copy of the American commissioners' passport document ever to appear at auction.

Christiaan Barnard and Curtis Bill Pepper
Christiaan Barnard, One Life
First edition, second printing, New York: Macmillan, 1970, octavo
New York $13,800 (£8,280)
26.VI.98

In December 1967 Dr Christiaan Barnard stunned the world with his announcement of the first successful human heart transplant. Dr Barnard's remarkable life and details of the momentous operation are recounted in his best-selling autobiography. This presentation copy has an elaborate pencil drawing on the front endpaper showing '*How to do a Transplant*', which is signed by Dr Barnard and dated *29 June 1971.*

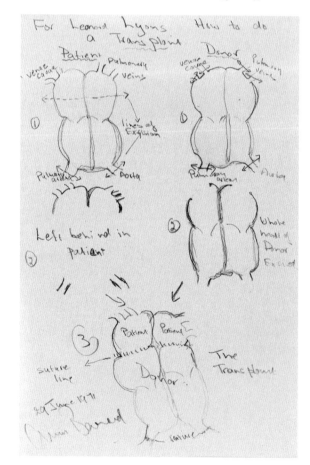

DECORATIVE ARTS

ISLAMIC ART

**An Iznik Polychrome
Pottery Border Tile**

Turkey, *c.* AD 1560
25 by 12 cm (9⅞ by 4¾ in)
London £43,300 ($70,146)
17.X.97

Tiles of this design were used
in the library of Ahmed I at
the Topkapi Saray Palace in
Istanbul. The *cintimani*
(triple roundels) motif, of
which the significance for the
Ottomans has not yet been
convincingly established, is
decorated in red, green and
cobalt-blue.

**An Abstract Ivory
Chess Piece**

Egypt, 10th/11th century
Height 8 cm (3⅛ in)
London £172,000
($287,240) 30.IV.98

In terms both of size and
quality this is one of the most
impressive of the abstract-
form chess pieces from the
Fatimid period. It represents
the 'bishop', the two conical
projections being the
typical means of depicting
this piece.

**An Emerald, Diamond,
Ruby and Sapphire-set
Enamelled Gold Necklace**
Morocco, c. 18th century
Length 31 cm (12¼ in)
London £84,000 ($136,080)
16.x.97

Lavishly set and beautifully
enamelled Moroccan
jewellery, such as this piece,
exerted a considerable
influence on leading Western
jewellers in the 1920s and
'30s and the 17th- and 18th-
century originals were highly
sought-after. A necklace
similar to this was in the
collection of Madame Elsa
Schiaparelli, one of this
century's most important
avant-garde fashion
designers.

A Safavid Brass *Kashkul*
Western Persia, c. AD 1580
38 cm (15 in)
London £188,500 ($305,370)
16.x.97
From the Hashem
Khosrovani Collection

This piece has been
identified as the earliest
example of a group of finely
and heavily cast bronze
kashkuls (symbolic begging
bowls), a style that appears
to have lasted from c. 1580 to
c. 1610. Its elegance of form
can be appreciated in purely
sculptural terms.

A Gupta Red Sandstone Head of Buddha
Uttar Pradesh, Mathura region, 5th century
Height 31.7 cm (12½ in)
New York $1,020,000 (£612,000) 26.111.98
From the Estate of Earl Morse

The Gupta dynasty, established in AD 320 in northern India, witnessed the high point of creative achievement in Indian art, and sculptures produced at that time are now considered the classic artistic expression of Buddhist art in India. The stylistic characteristics found in Gupta sculptures were exported to both Southeast and East Asia and profoundly influenced later Buddhist art. Two main schools dominated the Gupta style and worked in different types of stone. That centred at Sarnath used buff-coloured sandstone; the other school, which originated near Mathura and from where this example comes, carved from red sandstone.

A Gilt-bronze Figure of the Dharmapala Mahakala
Imperial China, mid 15th century
Height 57.8 cm (22¾ in)
New York $690,000
(£414,000) 26.iii.98

This important sculpture is said to have originally come from the Imperial Summer Capital of Jehol (Chengde), north of Peking, where it was purchased by Swedish explorer Sven Hedin (1865–1952). This image was acquired during his 1928–33 expedition to China, and was bought, with several other pieces, on behalf of Vincent Bendix, chairman of the Bendix Corporation of Chicago. The sculpture was exhibited in Chicago and at the 1939 World's Fair in New York, but in 1940 was sold to the Archeological Trust of Chicago, which subsequently donated it to Oberlin College, Ohio. In 1964 most of the former Bendix collection was acquired by a member of Hedin's original expedition for the Ethnographic Museum in Stockholm. The Mahakala however was missed and was only rediscovered in 1986 beneath a pile of timbers from the replica temple in which it had been housed.

CHINESE WORKS OF ART

A Falang Cai Vase
Mark and period of Qianlong
(1736–95)
Height 20.3 cm (8 in)
Hong Kong HK$9,920,000
(£768,992; $1,281,654)
5.XI.97

Like most pieces painted in the Imperial Palace Workshops in Beijing, this vase is unique. The golden pheasant depicted here was a popular subject of flower-and-bird painting and had been adopted by the Italian Jesuit painter, Giuseppe Castiglione, when he was installed as a court painter. The exquisite detailing of the pheasants' plumage and the shrubs is only found in porcelain belonging to this very rare group where short poems are added to the decoration and the marks are written in blue enamel.

A 'Tobacco-leaf' Dinner Service
Qianlong (1736–95)
London £397,500 ($651,900)
17.VI.98

This dinner service was purchased by a director of the East India Company who lived at Moor Park, Hertfordshire. Having started out as an apprentice cabinet-maker, he came to acquire at least 14 East Indiamen. Upon his death the service was passed to his son and thence by descent. Each piece is decorated with flowers issuing from amidst large overlapping tobacco leaves. This pattern is the most sought-after by today's collectors and it is rare to find such a complete set. It achieved a world record for a single Chinese Export dinner service.

A Blue and White Basin

Ming Dynasty, Yongle period
(1403–24)
Diameter 34.9 cm (13¾ in)
London £353,500 ($597,415)
2.XII.97

The shape of this basin follows an Islamic prototype seen in the brass basins from Iran, Syria and Egypt, which are often even larger. Although much of China's porcelain production in the early Ming Dynasty was made for the Middle Eastern market, it is a curious fact that vessels of foreign inspiration such as this seem to have been destined for the Chinese court, perhaps for Muslims engaged there. In their designs the porcelain painters did not follow the metal basins, which are usually decorated with calligraphic motifs, but the formal hexafoil rosette inside the bowls is based on Middle Eastern patterns. This example forms an identical 'pair' with a Qing basin, the only one currently recorded.

A Set of Twelve 'Famille-verte' Month Cups

Marks and period of Kangxi
Height 5.4 cm (2⅛ in)
New York $706,500
(£438,030) 23.IX.97

Each of these cups is illustrated with a different plant emblematic of each month of the year and is inscribed with a couplet by a Tang poet relating to the scene. For example, the sixth month shows a pair of mandarin ducks in a lotus pond and a kingfisher in mid-air with the poem *'Gen shi ni zhong yu. Xin cheng lu xia zhu'* ('Its roots are like pieces of jade in the mud. Its heart contains dewdrops like pearls').

One of a Pair of Gilt-bronze Figures of Guardians
Ming Dynasty, 15th century
Height 112 cm (44 in)
London £392,000
($638,960) 16.VI.98

It is rare to find a pair of guardian figures of such an elaborate type and impressive size. Each is finely cast and clad all over in layered chain-mail. The fierceness of expression is reinforced by the appearance of monster masks on the armour, for example, on the belly and arms of the guardian illustrated.

An Archaic Bronze *Lei*
Western Zhou Dynasty
Height 44.8 cm (17⅝ in)
New York $288,500
(£172,754) 23.III.98

Lei of this impressive type with dense overall decoration are rare but a group of similar vessels has been excavated at Qijiacun, Fufeng county, in Shaanxi province. Produced during the Zhou Dynasty (1027–221 BC), which favoured abstract designs, this vessel is unusual for the anthropomorphic flavour of its decoration, seen in the appearance of dragons around the sides and water buffalo heads at the handles.

A Carved Tianhuang Figure of Budai

Signed, Yang Yuxuan, 17th century
Width 6.1 cm (2⅜ in)
Hong Kong HK$2,000,000
(£153,965; $258,398)
28.IV.98

The deep honey-yellow stone of this laughing, corpulent figure of Budai is the most prized type of soapstone found in China. The reverse is signed by the artist Yang Yuxuan from Fujian province who was one of the most influential carvers of his day.

An Imperial Songhua Inkstone with Peking Enamel Box

Marks and period of Kangxi (1662–1722)
The box 10 cm (4 in) long
Hong Kong HK$2,880,000
(£223,255; $372,093) 5.XI.97
From the Wah Kwong Collection

It is as rare to find Peking enamel wares of Kangxi mark and period as it is to find contemporary Songhua inkstones bearing the same mark. Only one comparable matching set, made in the Forbidden City but by different Imperial Palace Workshops, is recorded. The Songhua stone, which takes its name from the river, is carved in a flat oval shape, with an aperture revealing an irregular piece of mother-of-pearl suggesting foaming waves to serve as a water well.

A Pair of Porcelain Snuff Bottles

Seal marks and period of Qianlong
Height 4.9 cm (2 in)
New York $107,000
(£64,200) 23.III.98

The miniature moonflask shape of these bottles is decorated in 'famille-rose' enamels with traditional landscapes on both sides. A banana-leaf border around the neck and lattice pattern at the foot are painted in gold over a rich iron-red.

JAPANESE WORKS OF ART

A Kakiemon Porcelain Model of a Horse
Late 17th century
Height 45.1 cm (17¾ in)
New York $838,500
(£503,100) 25.III.98
From the Jakob Goldschmidt Trust Collection

Kakiemon figural models are first documented in a European collection in the 1688 inventory of Burghley House, Lincolnshire; however, records from the Dutch East India Company indicate that Japanese porcelain was exported to Europe as early as 1659. Fragile and difficult to ship,

Kakiemon figures were highly prized and rare additions to affluent European households. The various models produced included animals, mythical beasts and human figures. Of the few known models of a horse, this example – one of only four known to exist – represents the most striking type.

Rimpa School
Pampas Grass
18th century
Pair of six-fold screens (one screen illustrated); ink, colour and gold on paper, mounted on brocade, each screen 165.7 by 361.9 cm (65¼ by 142½ in)
New York $123,500 (£75,335) 25.IX.97

The last great flowering of Japanese art took place during the Edo period (1615–1868). The works produced by the Rimpa School thoughout this period derived their inspiration from nature and literature. Here, the slim, curving forms of the pampas grass are vividly portrayed against a gold background.

Kitagawa Utamaro
A Beauty With a Cat
Signed *Utamaro ga*, with
publisher's mark
Woodblock print, 38.7 by
26.1 cm (15¼ by 10¼ in)
London £155,500 ($259,685)
30.x.97
From the Henri Vever
Collection

In October 1997 the fourth
and final part of the Vever
Collection was sold at
Sotheby's London. A leading
figure in the development of
Art Nouveau jewellery design
and production, Henri Vever
was a discerning and
voracious collector of art.
His collection of Japanese
prints, which included many
masterpieces of the genre,
was arguably the finest of its
kind ever assembled. This
example depicts a young
woman folding a length of
transparent material who
looks down indulgently at a
cat playing with the ends of
the cloth. The exceptional
state of colour preservation
reveals the skill and subtlety
of the colour printer who
uses three shades of purple
to render the transparency of
the material.

KOREAN ART

An Inlaid and Incised Celadon Bowl
Koryo Dynasty, 12th century
Height 8.6 cm (3⅜ in),
diameter 16.4 cm (6½ in)
New York $90,500 (£55,205)
26.ix.97
From the Estate of Marcus W. Scherbacher

This celadon bowl is a classic example of the refined aesthetics and technical achievement of the Koryo Dynasty (10th–14th century). Its unusual 'relaxed' contour shape features a design of peonies, a symbol of prosperity and wealth. The combination of fine incising on the exterior balanced by black and white slip-inlay technique on the interior is also rare. This piece featured in the sale of Korean art from the Estate of Marcus W. Scherbacher, who was the American Cultural Attaché in Korea from 1945 to 1958.

A Tairona Gold Figural Pendant

c. AD 1000–1500
Height 13.3 cm (5¼ in)
New York $563,500
(£332,465) 24.XI.97

Tairona goldwork includes some of the most skillful lost-wax casting done by ancient metallurgists in the Pre-Columbian world. The mastery of technique is complemented by a love of detail, seen in the extensive use of decoration and range of subject matter. This finely cast figure of an alligator-headed deity – one of the largest of its type – wears free-moving earrings and a massive headdress with two toucans perched on top. Its flared nostrils, furrowed brows and imposing attire make this a powerful and dramatic representation of a mythical creature.

A Benin Bronze Plaque
c. 16th century
45.1 by 34.9 cm (17¾ by
13¾ in)
New York $321,500
(£192,200) 6.v.98

Originally from the royal
residence in Benin, this
plaque of two officials in full
court regalia was collected by
an officer on the British
Punitive Expedition in 1897.
The palace was the location
of one of the most prolific
and fascinating forms of
Benin art. It was on the
palace walls that the now
famous rectangular brass
plaques, whose relief images
portray the persons and
events that animated court
life, were displayed. The
plaques depicted battles as
well as ceremonial life in the
palace, including the
costumes, ornaments and
weapons that conferred
status and a specific role on
to the wearer. The officials
realized here wear a single
feather over the left ear –
the white tail feather of the
fish-eagle, *oghohon* – which
was worn by chiefs at
ceremonial occasions to
symbolize their high status,
achievement and purity.

AMERICAN INDIAN ART

A Hopi Polychrome Wood Kachina Doll
Height 45.7 cm (18 in)
New York $294,000
(£173,460) 4.XII.97
From the Alan Kessler Collection

The Kachina, ancestral spirits in American Indian mythology, were invoked at religious ceremonies by dancers dressed to represent them. Carved from the root of the cottonwood, the Kachina dolls would be made by a young girl's maternal uncle in seclusion in the *kiva*, his clan's half-underground room, and then presented to his niece through a living Kachina at the end of a ceremony. The production of a Kachina-figure is, according to the Hopi, an act that needs to be done in the right manner and with a pure heart. This example of a dancing Shalako Mana, probably dating from before 1890, is unusual for an early piece in that it indicates the sex of the female spirit through the triangular genital area. The figure is decorated with red and white body paint and wears a sack mask and *tableta* headdress, which is a representation of clouds.

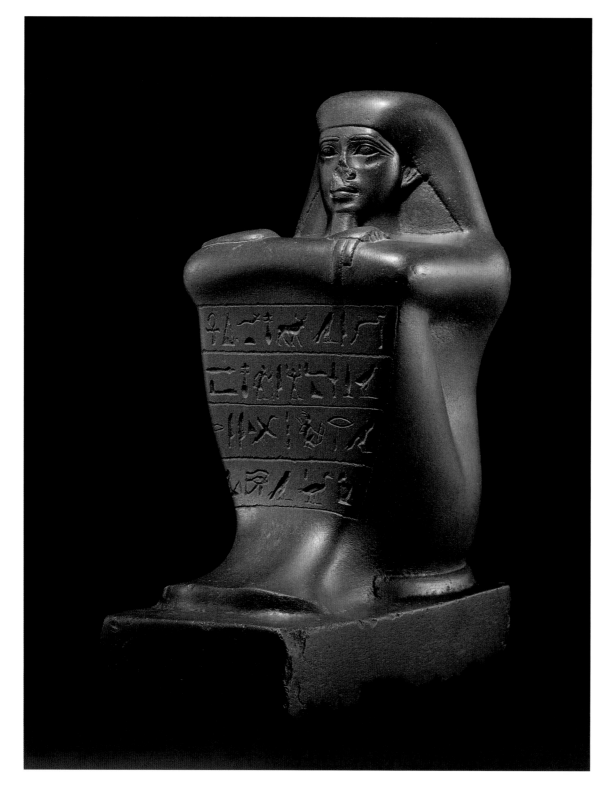

An Egyptian Basalt Block Statue of General Pa-Kyr
26th Dynasty
Height 31.4 cm (12⅜ in)
New York $684,000
(£417,545) 17.XII.97
From the Barratt-Brown
Collection, formerly in the
collection of Omar Pacha
Sultan

The statue of Pa-Kyr, a
general of the 26th Dynasty
(664–525 BC), reflects the
continued strength of
Egyptian art at the beginning
of the Late Period. The style
is elegant, understated and
deceptively simple, with the
blocky forms common to this
type of statue transformed by
balanced curves. The only
clue to Pa-Kyr's identity is
given in the hieroglyphs,
where he is named as
'overseer of the army'
(equivalent to the modern
rank of general). He served
under Psamtik I (664–610
BC), the first ruler of the
26th Dynasty.

EUROPEAN WORKS OF ART

A Florentine Bronze Pacing Lion
After Giambologna, attributed to Gianfrancesco Susini, second quarter 17th century
Height 13.3 cm (5¼ in)
New York $68,500 (£41,785)
29.1.98

This composition derives from the so-called Medici Lion, which was excavated in Rome in the 1580s and was acquired by Grand Duke Ferdinand I for the Villa Medici. Giambologna and Antonio Susini, his chief collaborator, were in Rome at this time, which could account for Giambologna's model being recorded in 1587 in the collection of Ferdinand I. A pacing lion is also recorded as one of the models in the studio of Gianfrancesco Susini who ran the Grand-ducal workshop after the death of his uncle Antonio, in 1624.

A French Terracotta Group of a Lion Savaging a Wild Boar
Edme Dumont, signed and dated 1768, height 36.8 cm (14½ in)
New York $28,750 (£17,538)
29.1.98

Remarkably few sculptures exist by Edme Dumont, who was elected to the Académie Royale in 1768 with his sculpture of the death of Milo of Crotona, now in the Louvre. Milo was a celebrated Greek athlete who attempted to tear an oak tree in two but the trunk closed over his hands and he was devoured by lions. The sculpture of Milo was executed in the same year as this terracotta and it is possible that the subject of the savage lion was a preoccupation with the artist at this time.

An English Painted Terracotta Bust of Edward Salter, Aged Six

Michael Rysbrack, inscribed on the sides of the base
ML RYSBRACK Fect: EDWARD SALTER AE(TA)TIS 6. 1748
Height 41.5 cm (16⅜ in)
London £279,050 ($457,642)
8.VII.98

Michael Rysbrack, born in Antwerp in 1694, was one of the younger sons of a landscape painter, Peter Rysbrack. He was apprenticed to the Antwerp sculptor Michael Vervoort and his name appears as Master of the Guild of Saint Luke in 1714. He came to England in around 1720 and soon achieved success, securing many important commissions from such patrons as Daniel Finch, 2nd Earl of Nottingham and 7th Earl of Winchilsea (see page 145). The present bust, previously unknown and undocumented, depicts the son of Anne and Thomas Salter, a clerk in the Board of Green Cloth at St James's Palace, the accounting office of the Royal Household. It retains the original paint applied by the artist, the purpose of which was to disguise the imperfections caused by firing the terracotta. Whilst giving strength to the material, firing caused cracks, variations in surface colour and other imperfections that the sculptor had to rectify before final delivery of his work.

CONTINENTAL FURNITURE

A Pair of French Gilt-bronze Mounted, Ebony, Jasper Topped, Porphyry and Pietra Dura Cabinets
The gilt-bronze mounts on each side with the device of the Dukes of Hamilton, first quarter 19th century, the pietra dura panels, French and late 17th century
103 by 67 by 38 cm (3 ft 4½ by 2 ft 2½ by 1 ft 3 in)
London, £958,500 ($1,571,940) 10.VI.98

These cabinets are reputed to have come from the collection of the great connoisseur William Beckford (1759–1844) or the 10th Duke of Hamilton, an avid collector of hardstones, whose arms appear on this piece. Beckford had connections to the Hamilton family of which he was very proud. His mother Maria was the granddaughter of James Hamilton, the Earl of Abercorn, and in 1810 his daughter, Susan Euphemia, married Alexander, 10th Duke of Hamilton. A sketch of one of the cabinets exists in the Beckford Archive at the Bodleian Library, Oxford but there is no record of them in the sales that dispersed the connoisseur's collection in 1839. It is likely that they were sold privately before that date, when Beckford was already in dire financial straits.

A Pair of Italian Bronze Groups Representing the Elements Fire and Air
Cast from models by Alessandro Algardi, 17th century
Height 1.17 m (46 in)
New York $1,322,500 (£793,500) 1.XI.97

Diego Velazquez travelled to Rome in 1640 to purchase works of art for Philip IV of Spain's palace at Aranjuez. On behalf of the king he commissioned Alessandro Algardi – whose reputation was then well-established – to produce fire-dogs symbolizing the Four Elements, the first two representing Jupiter (Fire) and Juno (Air) and the second two Neptune (Water) and Cybele (Earth). This pair, depicting Jupiter victorious over the Titans and Juno controlling the winds, were formerly in the Collection of the Duke of Westminster and are similar in composition to the single-gilt fire-dog of Juno in the Louvre. Jupiter has been identified with another model that stood in 1862 in one of the four niches of the Salon Ovale at Versailles.

**A German Transitional
Gilt-bronze Mounted Bois
Satiné, Stained Boxwood
and Marquetry Bureau
à Cylindre**
c. 1775–79, David Roentgen
118 by 108 by 67 cm (3 ft 10½
by 3 ft 6½ by 2 ft 2½ in)
London £353,500 ($593,880)
3.XII.97

David Roentgen (1743–1807)
was the most celebrated
German cabinet-maker, and
certainly one of the most
skilled ébénistes, of the 18th
century. He began working in
Neuwied in Germany but
was determined to move to
Paris, setting up a shop there
in 1781. He soon developed

an illustrious international
clientele; Louis XVI and
Queen Marie Antoinette, the
comte d'Artois and Catherine
the Great were amongst
those who praised his
furniture, the latter
remarking, 'His furniture is
very finely made, especially
those pieces with mechanical

devices'. The present bureau
has always been part of
important collections, most
notably that of Baron Lionel
Nathan de Rothschild, who
bought Tring Park in
Hertfordshire in 1872,
and his son Nathaniel.

A Pair of Louis XV Ormolu Three-light Appliques
Attributed to Caffiéri
Height 60 cm (23⅝ in)
Monaco FF914,500 (£82,835; $150,164) 27.VI.98

Jacques Caffiéri (1678–1755) was the son of an Italian wood carver. By 1714 he was a master carver and a few years later his name appears on the royal accounts. Although it is impossible to identify particular works in these accounts, it is almost certain that Caffiéri was responsible

for making items for the palace of Versailles. Many wall lights such as this pair are listed in an inventory of stock taken on his death in 1755 but, once again, the document is too vague to definitively attribute the design to Caffiéri.

A Louis XV Gilt-bronze Wall Clock
The bronzes signed *St. Germain*, the dial and movement signed *HERBAULT À PARIS*
Height 100 cm (39⅜ in)
Monaco FF1,239,000 (£112,228; $203,448) 27.VI.98

This clock is adorned with cherubs, garlands of flowers and acanthus leaves and is surmounted by the figure of Diana and one of her hunting dogs. There are several well-known versions of clocks of this design but with the cherubs differently positioned or omitted

altogether. This particular version is recorded on St Germain's stock inventory, which was taken in 1747 following the death of his first wife and was conducted by the master founders Thomas Oblet and François Gilbert.

A Pair of Louis XVI Ormolu Three-light Bras de Lumière
c. 1780, each stamped with the letter F Crowned, No. 34 3
Height 88.9 cm (35 in)
New York $1,157,500
(£694,500) 1.XI.97

This pair of wall lights, delicately adorned with sprays of roses, lilies, acanthus leaves and berried branches, were originally part of a three-pair set. The other two, acquired in 1865 by the Marquess of Hertford, are in the Wallace Collection in London. Four of the wall lights from the original set decorated the walls of Louis XVI's bedroom at Compiègne before being moved on 16th August 1786 to Queen Marie Antoinette's grand cabinet or *salon des jeux* at Fontainebleau. All three pairs were listed in a 1788 Fontainebleau inventory and, in 1794, were reserved by the Commission du Commerce as objects of value and transported to Paris. The history of the wall lights in the years between their removal to Paris and the acquisition of two of the pairs by the Marquess of Hertford in 1865 has not yet come to light.

ENGLISH FURNITURE

A Pair of George III Blue John and Gilt-brass-mounted Candelabra
Matthew Boulton, c. 1775, 37.5 by 40 cm (1 ft 2¾ in by 1 ft 3¾ in)
London £287,500 ($471,500)
10.VII.98

This magnificent pair of 'winged vases' established a new world record for blue john when sold in London. The vases correspond to a drawing preserved among the papers of Matthew Boulton who established his celebrated metalwork factory at Soho near Birmingham in the 1760s, producing silver, ormolu, blue john and other precious materials for such distinguished patrons as George III and Catherine the Great.

An Anglo-Chinese Rosewood Tilt-top Tripod Table
Second half 18th century,
76.2 by 77.5 cm
(30 by 30½ in)
New York $184,000
(£108,560) 17.IV.98

This table is a rare example of Chinese cabinet-making using a contemporary English example as a basis for its design. Almost certainly conceived for an English patron, the construction is wholly oriental, with the use of dry joints and small pegs, and the absence of secondary woods. The decoration is entirely English in character, as are the talon toes, but the carving has a certain softness and fluidity that is found on contemporary Batavian chairs in ebony and rosewood. The English character of the table suggests that it was made in Canton, the main trading port for English merchants in China.

A Set of Eight George II Walnut Dining Chairs
c. 1740, in the manner of
Giles Grendey, each back rail
stamped *WF* (one from the
set illustrated)
New York $211,500
(£124,785) 17.iv.98

Giles Grendey (1693–1780),
furniture-maker and timber
merchant, is probably best
known for the suite of gilt-
decorated scarlet japanned
furniture he produced for the
Duke of Infantado at Lazcano
Castle in northern Spain.
Like the Infantado chairs,
the back rails of this set
have the impressed initials
of a journeyman; chair
makers in Grendey's
workshop usually stamped
the rails with their initials.

A Pair of William and Mary Ebonized Beechwood Armchairs

c. 1689
London £210,500 ($345,220)
10.VII.98

These chairs were originally part of a larger suite of furniture comprising a bed, eight armchairs, four side chairs and a pair of stools, which were made for Daniel Finch, 2nd Earl of Nottingham and 7th Earl of Winchilsea (1647–1730), for the State Bedroom at Cleveland House, St James's. Finch was born into a family that had long been involved in politics and, for a time, he too played a prominent role in the affairs of the country, advising William and Mary. The design for the chairs, which proudly display an Earl's coronet, is indebted to the published work of Daniel Marot, which heavily influenced English craftsmen during this period. The grandeur and quality of the suite as a whole indicate the work of a prominent chair-maker such as Thomas Roberts who supplied furniture to the Royal Household. A fire in 1908 destroyed four of the armchairs and one of the side chairs; the State Bed, two armchairs and two stools are now in William and Mary's Palace at Het Loo. All remaining pieces retain their original Italian, probably Genoese, cut velvet covers and hangings, possibly acquired by Finch.

A Silk Embroidered Picture: The Tree of Life
Morris family, Philadelphia, late 18th century
New York $288,500
(£175,985) 19.1.98

The fashion for silk-on-silk embroidery featuring flowers and foliage, and occasionally birds and beasts, prevailed in colonial Philadelphia, and this example, a masterpiece of girlhood art from the city, is the fourth and best preserved 'tree of life with lion and leopard' embroidery to have emerged on to the market, having been previously unknown to scholars. Although the needlework does not bear the name of its maker, there is little doubt that Ann Marsh, a particularly accomplished schoolmistress, was responsible for the 'tree of life with lion and leopard' pattern, on which this is based. Embroidered by one of the former owner's great-great-grandmothers, this precious piece of Americana descended through the family for many generations. Of particular note are the curling branches, foliage and full-blown blossoms, which are in perfect harmony with Philadelphia's greatest expression of Rococo ornamentation.

Bill Traylor
Blue Man, Black Mule
Pencil and gouache on
cardboard, 38.1 by 65.7 cm
(15 by 25⅞ in)
New York $178,500
(£103,315) 3.XII.97
From the Collection of Joe
and Pat Wilkinson

Montgomery, Alabama artist
Bill Traylor spent the latter
days of his life seated on a
wooden bench in front of a
local pool hall quietly drawing
and painting a rich array of
pictorial subjects. Interiors,
religious gatherings, farm
activities, conflicts, human
and animal forms, fantastic
creatures and solitary
figures, as well as abstract
compositions, were all vividly
transposed from memory to
paper. Prior to beginning his
artistic career at the age of 85,
Traylor, who was born into
slavery, worked as a field hand
on a plantation outside
Montgomery. *Blue Man, Black
Mule* is a recollection of those
earlier days, transposed on to
cardboard with an economy
of line and gesture, and a
purity of colour.

Morris Hirshfield
*Nude with Hairbrush
(American Beauty)*
Signed and dated 1942
Oil on canvas, 121.9 by
101.6 cm (48 by 40 in)
New York $123,500 (£75,335)
18.1.98

Women and animals were
Morris Hirshfield's favoured
subjects and this depiction
of a sensual nude is a
primary example of the
self-taught artist's style.
Hirshfield spent the majority
of his life manufacturing
women's garments, which
possibly inspired the
intricately designed fabrics
that feature in his paintings.
Here, detailed drapery
provides a frame for the
sitter. Symbols relating to the
artist's religious background
often appear in his work;
reference can be found in
this painting in the colours
chosen for the curtains,
which are those of Zion's
flag. Hirshfield's imaginative
works placed him at the
forefront of the American
folk art movement in the
1940s and his work remains
highly appreciated today.

**A Queen Anne Carved,
Parcel-gilt, Figured Walnut
Bonnet-top High Chest of
Drawers**
Boston, Massachusetts,
1730–50
2.26 by 1.07 m
(7 ft 5 in by 42 in)
New York $937,500
(£571,875) 18.1.98

A masterpiece of early
Boston furniture, this high
chest displays drawers faced
by brilliant walnut crotch
veneer with the flame figure
deliberately chosen to centre
the upward rhythm of the
engraved brasses. Other
features that delight the eye
include the mouldings at the
arch top and waist, the inlaid
herringbone borders of the
drawer fronts, the painted
shells and the fluted and
gilded flame finials. It is one
of a small group that share
design qualities with a
signed high chest by the
Charlestown cabinet-maker
Ebenezer Hartshorn dated
1739, now at the Museum of
Fine Arts, Boston. Like the
present piece, the Hartshorn
chest achieves a rich
interplay between micro
and macro visual effect
through the juxtaposition of
walnut crotch veneer on the
drawer fronts with subtle,
contrasted areas of
decoration.

A Federal Satinwood-inlaid and Figured Mahogany Demilune Games Table

Labelled John Seymour & Son, Creek Square, Boston, Massachusetts, 1794–96
72.7 by 91.4 by 91.4 cm (28⅝ by 36 by 36 in) with table open
New York $541,500 (£330,315) 18.1.98
Property of Claire Beckmann

Claire Beckmann, schoolteacher and yard sale enthusiast, purchased this games table for $25 at a yard sale in Bergen County about 30 years ago. Since the discovery of the first piece of furniture with a Seymour label in the 1920s there has been much interest in the father and son's work. The present example, one of only six known labelled pieces, forms a pair with a games table in a private collection; both are masterpieces of design, craftsmanship and wood choice, with a level of sophistication rarely equalled in the Federal period. The Seymours' labour intensive (and expensive) craftsmanship was apparently not suited to the market for, by 1799, they were described by Boston's assessors as 'poor'.

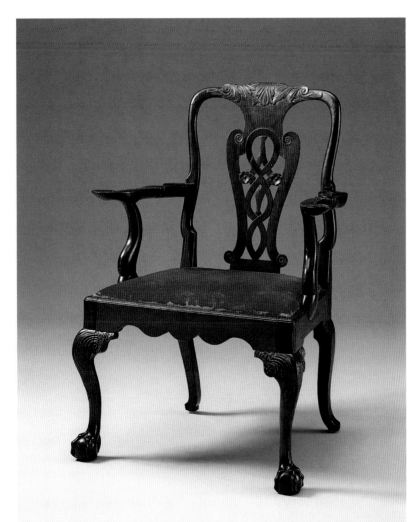

A Queen Anne Carved and Figured Mahogany Open Armchair

Attributed to the Edenton School, Albermarle, Edenton Area, North Carolina, 1745–50
Height of seat 45.7 cm (18 in), height of crest 1 m (39½ in)
New York $233,500 (£144,135) 9.x.97

Few examples of high style furniture from 18th-century Southern America have survived. This armchair is one of four of its type known to exist: the other three are in the Museum of Early Southern Decorative Arts in Winston-Salem. The comparatively recent attribution of the group to the 'Edenton School' has led to a reassessment of Southern furniture, for the chairs show a remarkable sophistication in transferring avant-garde designs to America at an early date.

NINETEENTH-CENTURY FURNITURE

A Louis XV Style Gilt-bronze Mounted Tulipwood Marquetry Side Cabinet by François Linke

Paris, 1900, modelled by Leon Messagé
144.8 by 144.8 by 73.7 cm
(4 ft 9 by 4 ft 9 by 29 in)
New York $574,500
(£344,700) 29.IV.98

The Paris 1900 *Exposition Universelle* marked a turning point in François Linke's career, establishing his reputation as a cabinet-maker. Linke's early work consisted mainly of copies of important 18th-century furniture, a common practice of the time, but that exhibited at the *Exposition* reflected a full awareness of and desire to express the new Art Nouveau style. Linke's success was due in no small part to his collaboration with sculptor Leon Messagé, about whom little is known. Their interpretation of the traditional Louis XV style of the 18th century, which incorporates the sinewy strength of Art Nouveau, was a highly innovative development in furniture design.

A Totara Knot and Boxwood Sideboard by Johann Martin Levien

Dated *1851*, carving by Sig Lovati
211 by 311 by 93 cm (6 ft 11 by 10 ft 2⅜ by 3 ft ¾ in)
London £309,500 ($504,485)
15.V.98

Born in Western Pomerania in 1811, Johann Martin Levien travelled widely and in 1837 set up a business in Brazil where he collected specimens of exotic woods from the interior. This passion for discovering materials led him to New Zealand in 1840 where he quickly became proficient in English and Maori. Levien specialized in exploiting the newly discovered timbers of the region, shipping many to England, including the wood used in this sideboard. Three years later Levien left to discover potential markets in Britain and business flourished: his clients included Baron Rothschild and Friedrich Wilhelm IV, King of Prussia. The present piece was produced for the *Great Exhibition* in 1851. It received honourable mention and was reported in accounts of the exhibition as one of the highlights.

NINETEENTH-CENTURY SCULPTURE

Charles Henri Joseph Cordier

The Jewess of Algiers and the Cairene Sheik: A Pair of Busts
Inscribed *Cordier* and
C. Cordier
Gilt-bronze, brown patina, onyx and enamel on red marble socles and pink granite columns with white marble foot and green marble plinth, overall height 215.9 cm (85 in)
New York $387,500
(£236,375) 23.x.97

Cordier's sculpture, which was collected by eminent patrons such as Queen Victoria, is distinguished by the rich juxtaposition of techniques and materials. Approximately 50 busts produced by the artist, many commissioned for the Musée d'Histoire Naturelle in Paris, represent a unique attempt to combine science and art in the form of ethnographic sculpture. In an effort to capture the ideal beauty particular to a race, Cordier overturned the canon of classical marble sculpting and developed a new aesthetic. This pair shows Cordier at his best, both in their materials, strikingly combining colour and texture, and their grandness of scale.

Francesco Barzaghi
Dea dei fiori (The Goddess of Flowers)
Signed, white marble, 210 cm (82¾ in)
London £183,000 ($300,120) 4.vi.98

Dea dei fiori is probably the most celebrated of Barzaghi's exhibition marbles. He is known to have shown this subject at the annual *Esposizione Nazionale di Belle Arti* twice, in 1878 and 1881. At the latter the marble was bought by Umberto I and lent to the Galleria d'Arte Moderna in Milan, where it remains today. It has been suggested that the 1881 sculpture was a second version of *Dea dei fiori*, distinct from the 1878 marble. The present marble is thus likely to be the earlier statue, since no other example is currently documented.

A Lund's Bristol Figure of Lu Tung-Pin
c. 1750–51, height 17.5 cm (6⅞ in)
New York, $43,125 (£25,444)
16.iv.98
Property of the Metropolitan Museum of Art

This figure of one of the eight Daoist Immortals is based possibly on a Chinese ivory but more likely on a blanc-de-Chine original of 1690–1710. Of the fewer than 15 examples recorded, this is one of the more crisply moulded and falls into the rarer group with underglaze manganese on the base, which was probably only present on the last versions. It is a product of the short-lived partnership of Benjamin Lund and William Miller in Bristol from 1749 to 1752, when the little factory merged with Worcester.

A Sèvres Biscuit Figure of Montesquieu from 'La Série des Grands Hommes'
c.1784, modelled by Clodion, height 43.5 cm (17⅛ in)
New York $101,500 (£60,900) 25.iv.98

The distinguished subject of this piece is one of the 23 large biscuit figures adapted at Sèvres by the sculptors of the monumental marble statues in 'La Série des Grands Hommes', commissioned by the French government in 1776. Charles-Louis de Secondat, baron de la Brède et de Montesquieu (1689–1755), was from an old military family of modest wealth. Trained as a lawyer, he sat in the Parlement of Bordeaux, and in 1721 published *Lettres persanes*, a satire on French legal and political institutions, which brought him instant notoriety. After travelling through Europe for several years, Montesquieu returned to France and, in 1748, published *De l'esprit des lois*, his masterpiece of political thought. Its argument for the freedom of the individual inspired the Declaration of the Rights of Man and significantly influenced the Constitution of the United States in 1787.

The Buckmaster Goblet

William Beilby,
Newcastle-upon-Tyne,
c. 1765, height 18.5 cm (7¼ in)
London £67,500 ($111,375)
18.XII.97

The coat-of-arms gracing this goblet has been identified as being that of either the Buckmaster or Buckminster families, both of which seem to have been well-established in the area around Spalding in Lincolnshire. The pair to this piece is in the collection of the Cecil Higgins Museum, Bedford. From the known examples, the Beilbys appear to have decorated very few polychrome armorial goblets and the Buckmaster Goblets are the only recorded surviving pair in existence.

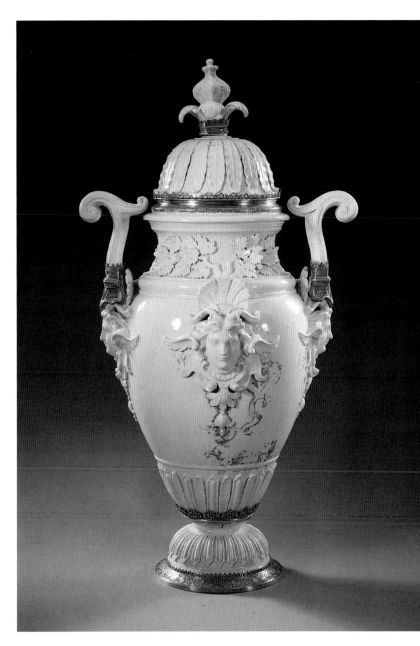

A Böttger Porcelain Silver-gilt-mounted Vase and Cover

c. 1717, modelled by Johann Jakob Irminger after a design by Raymond de Leplat, masks by Christian Kirchner, height 66 cm (26 in)
London £199,500 ($325,185)
14.VII.98

This vase is the largest and most important example of Böttger porcelain ever to be offered at auction and the only known example of this rare form to be mounted with handles. It is the central vase of a group of seven presented in 1725 by Augustus the Strong to his friend Vittorio Amadeo II, King of Sardinia, and is the only known design for the Meissen manufactory by the influential architect and artistic advisor to the Dresden Court, Raymond de Leplat.

A Lalique *Cire Perdue* Glass Figure of a Standing Maiden
c. 1905, white glass with sepia patina
Height 45.1 cm (17¾ in)
New York $288,500
(£175,985) 12.VI.98

The manufacturing of large, lost-wax statuary in glass was extremely challenging technically for Lalique, considering the rudimentary conditions of the studio in his country house at Clairfontaine, near Paris. The three extant *cire perdue* glass figures of standing maidens, of which this previously unrecorded example is undeniably the most successful, were achieved at Lalique's earliest point of transition from jeweller to glassmaker, and may be inspired by silver and ivory figures produced from 1902 to 1905. The alabaster-like quality of this figure, which enhances the classical form and adds an ethereal nature to the maiden, was achieved by the crystallization of the glass during the cooling stage. The addition of the sepia patina further heightens this quality.

A Pair of Five-light Candelabra

Designed by Josef Hoffmann and executed by Adolf Erbrich for the Wiener Werkstätte, before 1905
Height 48.5 cm (19⅛ in)
London £25,300 ($42,251)
31.X.97

Josef Hoffmann, architect and designer, co-founded the Wiener Werkstätte with Koloman Moser in 1903. The aim of the Vienna-based studio was to produce high-quality, handcrafted items, from metalwork to furniture and jewellery, that were affordable by the public. The finest productions of the Werkstätte, however, were special commissions, such as these candelabra, which were hand-wrought in silver. They are stamped with the monograms of the Wiener Werkstätte, the designer and the maker and were given by the sister of Karl Wittgenstein, a patron of the studio, to her daughter on the occasion of her marriage in 1905.

CARPETS AND RUGS

A Cheleberd Rug
Southwest Caucasus, *c.* 1800
178 by 143 cm (5 ft 10 in by
4 ft 8 in)
London £89,500 ($149,465)
29.v.98
From the Bortz Collection

The rug illustrated here is
part of a small group of four
known related weavings; of
the other three, one is in the
Victoria and Albert Museum,
the other two in private
collections. All feature a field
design that is a development
of the 18th-century
Caucasian 'floral' carpets,
which includes complete
pendant palmette motifs
supporting a main
medallion, flanked by large
hooked leaves and plants.
These four weavings provide
the only physical evidence for
the transition of the design
between the large 18th-
century carpets and the
Caucasian 'Cheleberd' rugs
of the 19th century.

A Pictorial Bessarabian Carpet
Dated and bearing the inscription *1846 JULIE 26 VOROTETZ*
4.24 by 2.74 m
(13 ft 11 in by 9 ft)
New York $112,500
(£67,500) 12.XII.97

A persuasively life-like Indian elephant and its handler grace the centre panel of this carpet. The exotic landscape that surrounds them, with its palm trees and hill fort, is suggestive of an oriental location; the carpet itself was produced in Bessarabia, an area of Eastern Europe that is now divided between Moldova and Ukraine.

TAPESTRIES

A Brussels Tapestry Depicting a Judgement Scene
Late 15th century
3.71 by 3.12 m (12 ft 2 in by 10 ft 3 in)
New York $167,500 (£102,175) 29.1.98
Property of the Detroit Institute of Arts, sold to benefit the Acquisition Fund

The inscription on this tapestry reads 'the heir of Egypt demanded fraudulently the bride of the Son of Man whom [i.e. the bride] the Supreme Judge forthwith declared to be, on the contrary, the Gift of Grace', the ambiguity of which has prompted much debate. In an article discussing the tapestry, Adele Weibel suggests that the scene depicts the Supreme Judge enthroned while pronouncing sentence. The protagonists stand before him; the Heir of Egypt (Egypt signifying the sinful world, and this figure therefore symbolizing the Lord of the World, the opposite of Christ) is restrained by a companion to the right; Rational Soul is brought forward by Gift of Grace, accompanied by Son of Man and Reward of Life. Weibel suggests that the tapestry represents the Soul being freed by the Supreme Judge from the power of the Lord of the World into the keeping of the Gift of Grace.

The Lady and the Unicorn, a 'Millefleurs' Allegorical Tapestry
Tournai, late 15th century
295 by 198 cm (9 ft 8 in by 6 ft 6 in)
London £128,000 ($209,920) 29.V.98

The mythical unicorn is traditionally shown as a white horse with a goat's beard and a short curved or long single horn, like a narwhal tusk, set in its forehead. The origins of the unicorn lie buried in the myths and fables of antiquity; the earliest reference seems to be in 400 BC by Ctesias, which links the creature with India. There are also references to it in the Old Testament and the Psalms. In medieval times it was supposed that the unicorn could only be subdued by the gentleness of a virgin and would come and lay its head in her lap. The depiction of the lady actually riding the unicorn, as seen here, is unusual.

PRECIOUS OBJECTS

JEWELLERY

An Art Deco Bracelet
Oscar Heyman, c. 1925
Length 18.5 cm (7¼ in)
Geneva SFr509,500
(£211,410; $344,250) 20.V.98

Three generations and a near century of innovative design and manufacture in New York attest to the enduring appeal of the American jeweller Oscar Heyman & Brothers. Sotheby's catalogue entry for this piece reunited the bracelet and its original design for the first time since it was made, more than 70 years ago.

A Sapphire and Diamond Necklace/Bracelet Combination
Harry Winston
New York $825,000
(£495,000) 30.X.97

Designed as a flexible, slightly graduating strand of foliate design, this piece is set with seven emerald-cut sapphires weighing approximately 115.00 carats and is completed by 137 pear-shaped and round diamonds weighing approximately 50.80 carats. The sapphire segment detaches to form a bracelet and one side segment can be removed to shorten the necklace.

A Gem-set and Diamond Sword Brooch
Length 5.8 cm (2¼ in)
St Moritz SFr25,300
(£10,498; $17,094) 18.11.98

The handle and blade of this brooch are formed of three fancy-shaped diamonds, whilst the hilt is enhanced by an emerald, rubies and rose-cut diamonds. An additional garland of stones runs around the blade.

A Collection of Diamond Dress Ornaments from the Russian Imperial Court

Second half 18th century,
length 38 cm (15 in)
New York $211,500
(£126,900) 9.IV.98
Property from the Estate of
Irma Adler

The collection of diamond
dress ornaments presented
here displays the glorious
legacy of Russia's imperial
court jewels at the height of
their magnificence in the
18th century. These would
have been made for a high-
ranking member of the court,
perhaps for Catherine the
Great herself, and worn sewn
throughout the bodice and
skirt of a gown in a pattern or
randomly, like so many stars.
Not only do the diamonds
create a dazzling display of
wealth, the forms may also
allude to the rank of their
owner, for some are
designed as tulips, which
were then among the rarest
of flowers. The attention
to detail of each flower type
indicates the preference for
naturalism in jewellery at
this time.

A Fancy Vivid Orange Diamond

New York $1,322,500
(£793,500) 30.X.97

This cushion-shaped
diamond of fancy vivid
orange colour weighs 5.54
carats and is of a rare type
IIa. Such diamonds are of an
exceptionally pure chemical
composition, consisting of
almost all carbon. Diamonds
in the orange hue range are
often darker and less
saturated in colour, with their
hue modified by a brownish
appearance. A diamond such
as this, the colour of which is
described as orange with no
modifying terms, is unusual,
as is its lightness and
intensity, characteristics
more commonly associated
with a fine sapphire or
spessartine garnet.

A Ruby and Diamond Necklace/Tiara

c. 1890
Overall length of necklace
42 cm (16½ in)
London £287,500 ($480,125)
18.VI.98
Property of the Rt Hon
the Lord Somerleyton
KCVO, JP, DL

This necklace is designed as a graduated row of 18 rubies each at the centre of a diamond set cluster, the five largest of which are accompanied by certificates stating that they originate from Burma (Mogok, Myanmar). The larger ten clusters are detachable to form a tiara, with the remaining eight forming a bracelet. The piece was originally the property of Phyllis de Bathe, who married Savile, First Baron Somerleyton in 1887.

The Jonker No. 7 Diamond

Harry Winston
New York $827,500
(£496,500) 30.X.97

In January 1934 Johannes Jacobus Jonker's team of diamond diggers unearthed what was then the fourth largest diamond in the world. The exceptionally white, 726 carat stone was purchased a year later in London by Harry Winston who gave the task of cutting it to Lazare Kaplan, a jeweller known for his knack of obtaining the maximum fire and brilliance in a gem. After four months of study Kaplan cut the stone into 12 diamonds: 11 emerald cuts and one marquise. Sotheby's has sold three stones from the original rough Jonker, the 40.46 carat Jonker No. 2, the 30.70 carat Jonker No. 4, and this stone, the 19.74 carat Jonker No. 7.

A Diamond Necklace and Earrings
c. 1840
Length 39 cm (15⅜ in)
London £254,500 ($425,015)
18.VI.98

Designed as a *rivière*, this necklace is composed of 42 graduated cushion-shaped diamonds; the largest, weighing 11.36 carats, is supported at the centre as a pendant. The accompanying pair of diamond pendent earrings are each collet-set with two cushion-shaped diamonds.

A Lapis Lazuli, Jade, Coral and Diamond Necessaire de Soir
Cartier, c. 1925, signed
London £32,200 ($53,744)
18.VI.98

A triumph of design, workmanship and colour combinations, this Cartier box is fitted with two compartments, a lipstick holder and a mirror. Its design reflects the influence of the arts of Asia in the West in the 1920s, as well as the use of materials indigenous to the area.

A Diamond Necklace
Cartier, signed,
length 35.5 cm (14 in)
New York $690,000
(£414,000) 30.X.97

A *rivière* of old European-cut diamonds graduates in size here to support a fringe of pear-shaped diamonds surmounted by additional old European-cut diamonds, mounted in platinum. The European-cut diamonds featured in this necklace have an approximate total weight of 110.50 carats, the pear-shaped diamonds 19.00 carats.

A Jadeite Ring
2.46 by 1.95 by 0.64 cm
(1 by ¾ by ⅜ in)
Hong Kong HK$2,220,000
(£170,900; $286,821)
29.IV.98

The curved rectangular plaque of jadeite in this piece was taken from an archer's ring. During the Qing Dynasty (AD 1644–1911), the archer's ring was prized both for its protection of the thumb when the arrow was released, and for its implication of social status and military supremacy.

Double-strand Jadeite Bead Necklace
Clasp by Cartier, c. 1925
Outer strand length 63.5 cm
(25 in)
Hong Kong HK$9,920,000
(£763,664; $1,281,654)
29.IV.98

From the turn of the century Cartier has been hailed as a master of modern style and daring creations. Pieces from the 1920s, such as this jadeite bead necklace, reflect the influence of Chinese culture and motifs on the firm. The necklace consists of 130 beads, graduating in size, and is completed by a platinum art deco clasp, set with a circular cabochon star sapphire.

An Aquamarine, Diamond and Moulded Glass Corsage Ornament
René Lalique, 1905–06, signed
London £89,500 ($149,465)
18.VI.98

Lalique was the undisputed genius of Art Nouveau jewellery, a man of great talent and versatility who succeeded in transforming jewels from mere forms of ornament into great works of art. From the mid 1890s his jewellery began to show a strong sculptural element combined with the fluid and sinuous lines of Art Nouveau. The ambition to extend his palette encouraged his experiments with enamel and his innovation of mixing precious and non-precious materials, such as the moulded glass used here.

A Pair of Emerald and Diamond Earclips
Bulgari, signed
Geneva SFr1,543,500
(£648,270; $1,050,197)
20.V.98

These emeralds are of a quality associated with the finest jewels of the Indian Mughal Empire, where gem-cutters possessed the courage and vision to reveal the natural beauty of the emerald bead.

A Natural Pearl and Diamond Necklace
Mounted by Cartier, Paris, c. 1925, length 40 cm (15¾ in)
Geneva SFr421,500 (£174,896; $284,797)
20.V.98

Many of Cartier's creations, as well as those from other jewellery houses, were featured in the 1925 Paris Exposition des Arts Décoratifs et Industriels. A tendency towards geometry, stylization and contrast of materials was prevalent, as is evident in the necklace illustrated here: the bold sculptural design juxtaposes the hardest gem, the diamond, with the near softest, the pearl.

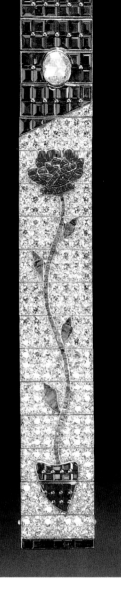

**A Diamond and
Tiara/Necklace
Combination**
c. 1930
Geneva SFr515,000
(£216,386; $367,857)
19.XI.97

This tiara is made from a
tapering band supporting
brilliant-cut diamonds held
by columns of cushion-
shaped and circular-cut
diamonds, mounted in
platinum. The upper section

of the tiara detaches, the
larger diamonds forming
an attractive *rivière*; the base
also detaches to form a
sautoir.

**A Symbolist Diadem and
the Original Design**
René Lalique, *c.* 1900
Diadem (design not
illustrated): 13.75 cm (5¾ in)
maximum width
Geneva SFr102,000
(£42,840; $72,400) 19.XI.97

The chance re-appearance
of two items on the market
within a very brief period
resulted in the rare
combination of a Lalique
jewel and the original design.
The 1993 purchaser of this
diadem bought the design

three months later thus
reuniting the two after a
separation of 90 years.

**The Tiffany 'Moonlight
Rose' Bracelet**
Tiffany & Co., signed, *c.* 1925,
length 17.8 cm (7 in)
New York $525,000
(£315,000) 9.IV.98

This bracelet is one of the
most important pieces of
American art deco jewellery
to be offered at auction. The
mosaic-like quality of the
lapidary work and the
arabesque curve of the rose
stem seem inspired by the
Islamic world, yet the red,
white and blue stones seem

to state an American theme.
The design is unprecedented,
since most of the important
pieces produced in America
in the 1920s followed
European styles. The
impeccable workmanship
may be that of William
Scheer, Inc. who
manufactured jewellery for
Tiffany & Co. and, while no
original sketches are known
to exist, a sketch for a
different rose bracelet by
Scheer betrays an exotic,
stylized naturalism similar
to that shown here.

A Tiara

Mario Buccellati, *c.* 1927
Milan L153,850,000
(£50,570; $84,386) 1.VI.98

Mario Buccellati was
apprenticed to Italy's
premiere goldsmiths at the
age of 12 and took over the
business in 1919. Success
was immediate and his fame
soon spread abroad with the
exhibition of his work at the
1921 Madrid *Exposition*,
during which he received a
visit from Spain's royal
family. His clientele came to
include the royal families of
Italy, Belgium and Egypt, the
Vatican Court and many of
the great personalities of the
day, such as the poet
Gabriele D'Annunzio. This
tiara, from a six-piece parure,
is one of a small number of
Buccellati's jewels in
existence dating from
1926–29. Jewels from this
period are much sought-after
for the way in which the art
deco style is rendered in a
19th-century setting.

Two Tassel Bracelets

Van Cleef & Arpels, *c.* 1930
Geneva SFr843,000
(£354,060; $573,577) 20.V.98

This highly sought-after
period design of the inter-
war years, produced in small
numbers, seldom appears
on the market, an example
of which figures in the Van
Cleef & Arpels own historic
Collection. Thus this pair,
sold separately, offered a
rare opportunity to
collectors.

A Gold and Diamond Bracelet

c. 1960
Milan L238,600,000
(£78,428; $130,872) 1.VI.98
From the Collection of
Renata Tebaldi

'Voce d'angelo', the voice of
an angel, was how Arturo
Toscanini described the
talents of soprano Renata
Tebaldi in 1946. The epithet
was appropriate: from the
late 1940s until her
retirement in 1976 Miss
Tebaldi was acclaimed
around the world for her
interpretation of the great
roles, becoming
affectionately known in
America as 'Miss Sold Out'.
Her collection of jewellery
was intimately connected
with her career, whether its
design was inspired by the
costume jewellery worn on
stage or bought as a
keepsake after a
performance.

CLOCKS AND WATCHES

A Gold Fusee Keyless Lever One Minute Tourbillon
Charles Frodsham,
No. 09133, AD Fmsz 1902
Diameter 5.7 cm (2¼ in)
London £45,500 ($73,710)
1.X.97

Charles Frodsham was one of the foremost watchmakers working around the turn of the century. The tourbillon carriage was a very difficult complication designed to eradicate any errors that may be brought about by changes to the position of the watch when it was worn.

A Pink Gold Tonneau Self-winding Perpetual Calendar Minute Repeating Wristwatch with Moon Phases and Retrograde Calendar
c. 1995, Patek Philippe & Co., Geneve, no. 1908029, ref. 5013
Diameter 3.5 cm (1⅜ in)
Hong Kong HK$1,780,000
(£137,028; $229,974)
27.IV.98

The matte silvered dial of this watch contains three apertures indicating day, month and leap-year cycle; the subsidiary seconds are combined with the phases of the moon. The heavy moulded tonneau case contains a 22-carat gold rotor and 21 jewels.

A George II Walnut Longcase Clock
Samuel Barkley & Thomas Colley, London, dated 1753
Height 244 cm (8 ft)
London £56,500 ($91,530)
1.X.97

Samuel Barkley was apprenticed to George Graham in 1715 and in time was elevated to the position of foreman; he was made a member of the Clockmakers' Company in 1722. Thomas Colley, although never formally apprenticed, was associated with Graham's workshop from an early age. Both men shared accommodation with George Graham and were executors of his last will and testament. They acknowledge the influence of their predecessor in the plaque on the front of this clock, which is inscribed 'Graham's Succs. Barkley & Colley, London'.

A Platinum Perpetual Calendar Tourbillon Minute Repeating Wristwatch with Moon Phases and Retrograde Calendar
c. 1995, Patek Philippe & Co., Geneve, no. 1905010, ref. 5016
Diameter 3.8 cm (1½ in)
Hong Kong HK$3,320,000
(£255,581; $428,940)
27.IV.98

Patek Philippe's principles of manufacturing, where every part of the watch is hand finished, have not changed over their 150 years of production. The company is credited with having created the most complex wristwatches in the world and the ref. 5016 is the most complicated to be produced

regularly. For the first time in watchmaking history, a tourbillon, minute repeater, perpetual calendar with fly-back date-hand and phases of the moon have been combined in a single timepiece.

A Gold Dual Crown World Time Wristwatch

c.1953, Patek Philippe & Co., Geneve, no. 722701, ref. 2523
Diameter 3.5 cm (1⅜ in)
New York $420,500
(£256,505) 9.iii.98

Louis Cottier invented and developed the world time system for Patek Philippe. The dual crown system was introduced as a modification to his first design, the manual system, which had been in use in the 1940s. Cottier's new development enabled the crown at 3 o'clock to rotate the inner chapter ring, and the crown at 9 o'clock to rotate the inner bezel, thus eliminating the necessity to hand-set the world time ring.

A Sympathique Clock

Breguet, no. 222
Overall height 33 cm (13 in)
Geneva SFr1,103,500
(£463,655; $788,214)
18.xi.97

In a letter to his son in 1795, Breguet describes his conception of the Sympathique as a means of enhancing his fame and fortune as the arch horological innovator. Three types were manufactured in the following 25 years. The earliest example zeros the minute hand at each hour. The next, of which no. 222 is an example, sets the minute hand and regulates the watch as necessary. This clock was sold in 1875 to SMI Le Grand Duke Constantin de Russie, the son of Tsar Nicholas I.

A Gold and Enamel Openface World Time Watch

c. 1945, Patek Philippe & Co., Geneve, no. 930365, ref. 605
Diameter 4.5 cm (1¾ in)
Geneva SFr168,500
(£69,917; $113,851) 19.v.98

The dial of this watch is of polychrome *cloisonné* enamel showing Neptune riding a seahorse. The surrounding chapter ring is divided into diurnal and nocturnal hours and for 24 hours; the outer silvered chapter ring is engraved with 42 world locations from Réunion to Denver, Tokyo to Fiji.

A Gold Hunter Cased Minute Repeating Split Second Chronograph Grande Sonnerie Clockwatch with Perpetual Calendar, Central Minute Register and Moon Phases

c. 1895, Audemars Piguet, no. 4091
Diameter 6.2 cm (2⅞ in)
New York $299,500
(£182,695) 27.x.97

Although it is curious that this high-quality example of Audemars Piguet's work does not have an obvious signature it is not unusual for the company at this time. Many watches made by the firm were either unsigned or, as in this case, stamped on the dial plate.

SILVER

The Conglomerate Vase
American silver and mixed-metal 'Japanese-Style' Exposition vase, Tiffany & Co., New York, 1878, signed
190 oz 10 dwt gross,
height 51.4 cm (20¼ in)
New York $585,500
(£357,155) 20.1.98

Eastern influences, which were very popular in the late 19th century, are apparent in the shape of this vessel, its design and the metalworking techniques used to produce it. The vase incorporates Japanese metallurgic processes, for example *mokume* (the appearance of wood graining) and the inlaying of other metals or alloys, such as *sentoku*, into silver. Vines with leaves and gourds are arranged asymmetrically on to a hammered silver ground, while paulownia leaves, the most popular image on Japanese Imperial crests, are applied to the base. These innovations were greatly admired by many who attended the 1878 *Exposition Universelle* in Paris, where the vase was exhibited.

**A German Royal Silver
Eight-light Chandelier**
Johann Christian Lieberkühn
after a design by Daniel
Marot, Berlin, c. 1710–20,
marked *ICL* in oval and
Berlin city mark
402 oz (excluding metal
rod), 61 by 78.7 cm
(24 by 31 in)
New York $1,982,500
(£1,189,500) 22.IV.98

Inspired for its principal
elements by a design of
Daniel Marot, this is the
only known surviving
chandelier by Johann
Christian Lieberkühn,
Court Goldsmith to Friedrich
Wilhelm I, King of Prussia.
Pieces by this celebrated
metalworker are rare, since
many of the silver
furnishings from the

Prussian court were melted
down. In 1745, 21 of 23
chandeliers made by
Lieberkühn were recast as
coinage by Friedrich II (the
Great) to pay for his wars in
Silesia, and melts were again
necessary in 1757 and 1809.
According to 18th-century
inventories, chandeliers of
this size, weight and number
of arms were used in private

rooms. Since the Marot
designs date from 1712, this
example may well have been
created in the second
decade of the 18th century,
and as the horses allude to
the Royal House of Hanover,
it was possibly a present
from Friedrich Wilhelm I
to his father-in-law, Georg
Ludwig, Elector of Hanover
and future King of England.

Eighteen George I Silver Plates

Anthony Nelme, London, 1719

323 oz, diameter 24.3 cm (9½ in)

London £166,500 ($273,060) 4.VI.98

Property of the Mellerstain Trustees

These 18 dinner plates were sold as part of a series of early English silver dishes that were made for George Baillie of Jerviswood and Mellerstain and sold for £797,100 ($1,307,244) on 4th June 1998. George was the son of Robert Baillie, a fervent Scots patriot who was executed for treason in Edinburgh in 1684. It was during his father's imprisonment that George met his future wife, the young Lady Grizel Hume. She was the eldest daughter of Sir Patrick Hume, a close friend of Robert Baillie, who, not daring to communicate directly with the imprisoned man, detailed the 12-year-old Grizel to deliver messages to the prison. Despite a period of financial ruin following Robert's execution, the Baillie family eventually prospered, an indication of which can be gained from the marvellous silver that they commissioned.

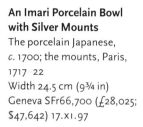

An Imari Porcelain Bowl with Silver Mounts

The porcelain Japanese, *c.* 1700; the mounts, Paris, 1717–22
Width 24.5 cm (9¾ in)
Geneva SFr66,700 (£28,025; $47,642) 17.XI.97

The majority of French silver-mounted porcelain dates from the late 17th and early 18th centuries. The Siamese Ambassador's visit to Versailles in 1686 began a fashion for oriental wares and the embellishment of porcelain through the addition of silver mounts reached a peak of popularity during the Régence (1715–23). Originally, much of the porcelain was supplied by the Dutch East India Company, but before long French traders were taking advantage of the huge demand and in 1700 the arrival of the *Amphitrite* was announced by the *Mercure de France*, with a cargo of 180,000 pieces of porcelain. By 1722 individual French ships were carrying up to 300,000 pieces.

A *Bartmannkrug* Stoneware Jug with German Silver-gilt Mounts

The ceramic Cologne or Frechen, the mounts maker's mark a housemark (Scheffler no. 2151), Cologne, *c.* 1550
Height 22 cm (8⅝ in)
Geneva SFr73,600 (£30,924; $52,571) 17.XI.97

The fashion in court circles for mounting German stoneware with silver and silver-gilt lasted from *c.* 1520 to 1580 and was principally an English one; German and Dutch beer drinkers normally fitted pewter mounts to the stoneware pots. Such lavish decoration to what would have been an inexpensive vessel came as a result of the regularity of their use; the sentimental value of such a common object led to them being personalized in such a luxurious manner.

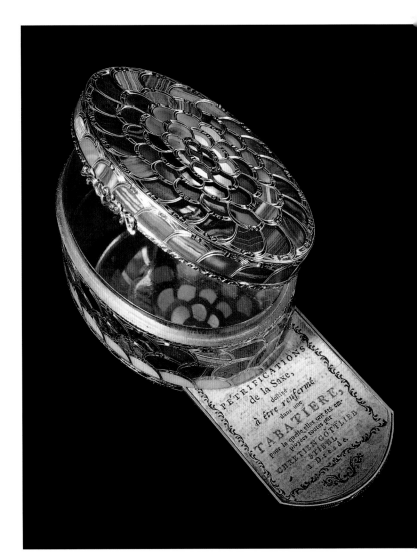

Empress Maria Feodorovna, née Princess Sophie Dorothea of Württemburg (1759–1828)
Attributed to Giovanni-Baptista Lampi, *c.* 1797
9.6 cm (3¾ in)
London £19,550 ($32,257)
5.III.98

Sophie Dorothea of Württemburg married the Tsareivich Paul Petrovitch in 1776 and assumed the name Maria Feodorovna upon her baptism into the Russian Orthodox Church. She endured her husband's many eccentricities and, following his assassination, built a cult of veneration for the 'martyred' Emperor.

A Fabergé Gold, Hardstone, Enamel and Jewelled Pansy
Worksmaster Henrik Wigström, St Petersburg, *c.* 1900
Height 4.5 cm (1¾ in)
New York $71,250 (£43,462)
11.VI.98

With his emphasis on craftsmanship and design, Carl Fabergé ensured that the value of objects produced by his company did not rest simply in their materials. This tiny flower bears out his maxim; the naturalistic, enamelled petals are centred by a diamond and the leaves are carved nephrite, bestowing a charming realism to the whole.

A Gold and Hardstone 'Steinkabinettestabatiere'
Christian Gottlieb Stiehl, Dresden, *c.* 1775
Width 8.5 cm (3⅜ in)
Geneva SFr608,500
(£255,672; $434,642) 18.XI.97

A concealed spring in the base of this box releases a tray which bears an explanatory printed booklet. In this are listed the places of origin of all 201 stones used in its making. It also provides an insight into the mind of an 18th-century gold box maker, for the introduction gives, in Stiehl's own words, his intentions in making the box and how he proceeded.

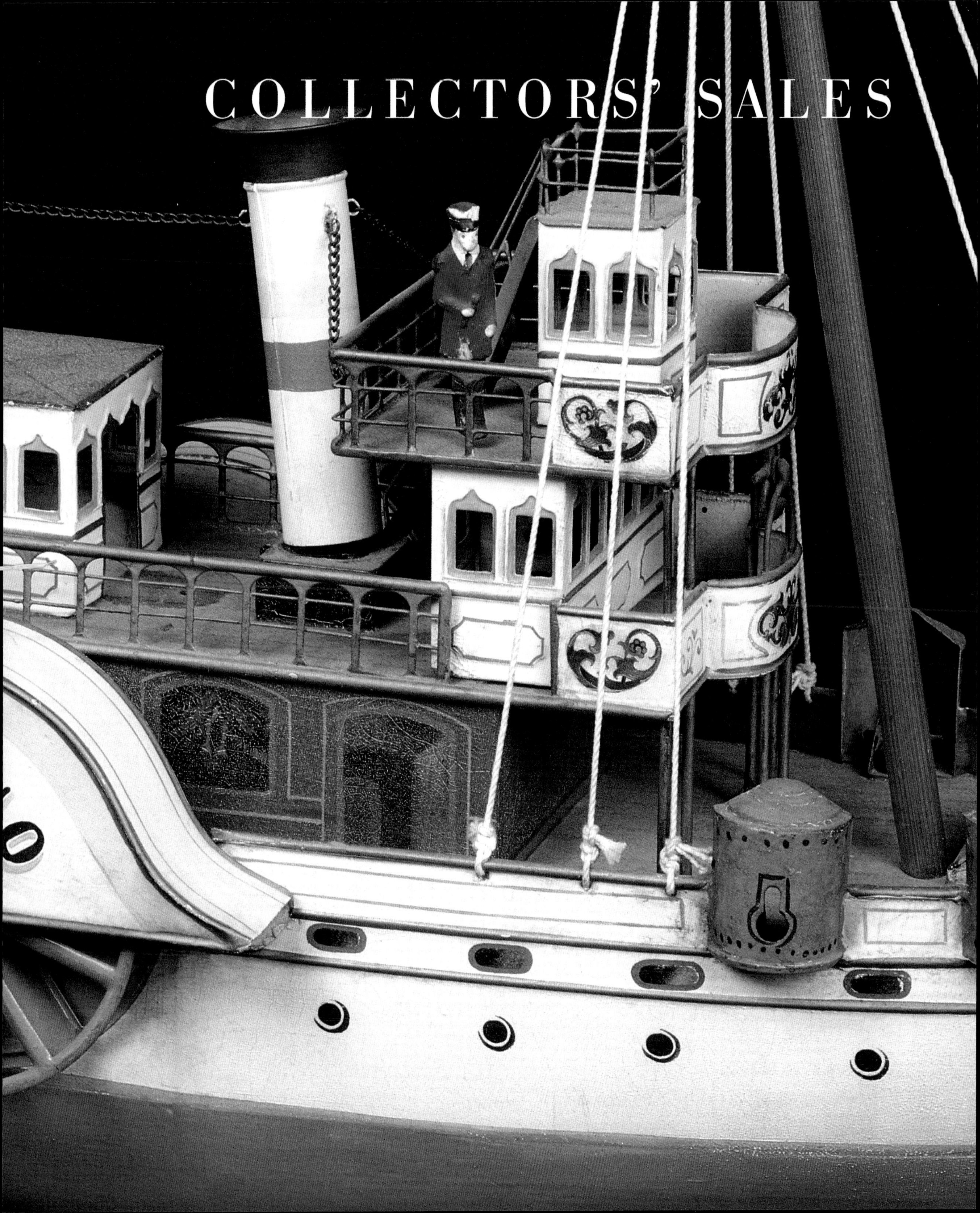
COLLECTORS' SALES

COINS, MEDALS AND STAMPS

Wreath Cent
United States of America, 1793
New York $93,500 (£57,035)
15.1.98

Among the first coins struck by the fledgling United States Mint, the wreath cent is considered to be one of the most beautiful designs ever produced. This example, among the finest known, exhibits qualities which indicate that it may have been intended for official presentation purposes.

Canada, 1868–71, 2c
London £2,185 ($3,583)
16.VII.98

Notable for its bright fresh shade of green, this block of four is a very rare example of a multiple of the Canadian 2c stamp.

Hankow, Nanking and Changsha, 1912, 1c to $5
Hong Kong HK$299,000 (£24,035; $38,680) 7.x.97
Sold in Association with Corinphila of Zurich

Of the eight pairs of these stamps sold, all retained their brilliant colours and were unused and unmounted. It is believed that they are the only unused multiple copies of high denomination stamps of this kind outside of official archives. The stamp illustrated is the $2 value.

Russia, Order of St Alexander Nevsky, c. 1910
Diamond-set sash badge, 5.23 cm (2⅛ in)
London £27,600 ($45,264)
7.VII.98

Founded in 1725, this order was awarded exclusively to high-ranking individuals for distinguished service. As an exceptional honour, it was occasionally awarded with diamonds. This example is from the collection of Ferdinand I, King of Bulgaria.

Prussia, Pour le Mérite
Neck badge in gold and enamel, with gold oak-leaf suspension, 8 cm (3⅛ in)
London £7,820 ($12,825)
7.VII.98

This order was bestowed upon Ferdinand I, King of Bulgaria as *Generalfeldmarschall der Preussischen Armee* on 8th September 1916.

Hindenburg Crash Covers
Right: franked with 75pf and 50pf adhesives, Berlin 3rd May 1937; below right: franked with one complete 25pf and a strip of five 40pf adhesives, 5th May 1937
New York $24,150 (£14,732)
3.III.98

These covers were recovered from the wreck of the airship Hindenburg which was destroyed by fire on 6th May 1937 at Lakehurst, New Jersey. That on the left was offered unopened, still sealed in an official envelope, exactly as it was delivered by the Post Office after the fire. The cover on the right bears two rare handstamps applied on board the airship.

ARMS, ARMOUR AND SPORTING GUNS

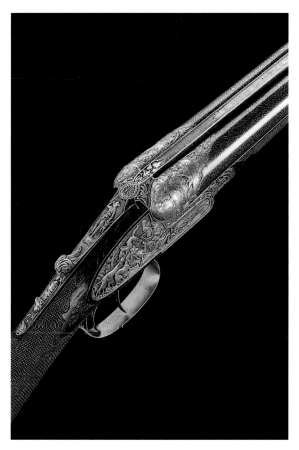

**H. Faure Lepage, A French
12-bore Sidelock Ejector Gun**
Chiselled and engraved by
J. G. Brun
London £27,600 ($46,092)
25.III.98

Frederic William Guillaume
Brun engraved this sporting
gun with images from
famous works by 18th-
century artists. The locks
depict scenes by Desports
and Oudry and the base of
the frame with the Miracle of
St Hubert from a work by
Dürer. The top lever is
engraved with the image of
Diana, goddess of hunting,
copied from a statue on
exhibition in the Louvre.

**A French Etched and Gilt
Model Armour for Man
and Horse**
In late-16th century style, by
E. Granger, Paris, c. 1850,
overall height 36.4 cm
(14⅜ in)
Sussex £25,300 ($41,998)
8.XII.97

The 19th-century Parisian
armourer E. Granger is
known to have made full-
sized armours, including
some for the waxwork figures
of Madame Tussaud and
others for use by the Paris
Opera, but it is for his model
armours that he is now

particularly admired. The
present example is of a
design that had already been
exhibited by him at the
*Exposition de l'Industrie
Française* in Paris in 1844.

A Three-keyed Boxwood Oboe by Joannes Hyacinthus Rottenburgh I
Brussels, first quarter 18th century
London £14,950 ($24,518)
17.XII.97
Property of Michel Piguet

This oboe was one of a group of 17 offered from the collection of the esteemed Swiss oboist Michel Piguet. Amongst his achievements, Piguet pioneered the performance of Baroque and Classical music on original instruments in this century. The maker of this example, Joannes Rottenburgh, is noted for successfully combining the disciplines of making both woodwind and string instruments.

The Pollitzer-Koessler
A Violin by Giuseppe Guarneri del Gesù, Cremona, 1736
London £551,500 ($932,035)
18.XI.97
Property of the Sam and Rie Bloomfield Foundation

Although not unique in Guarneri del Gesù's output, the use of maple cut 'on the slab', instead of 'on the quarter', is certainly a most unusual and striking feature of the back of this violin. The maker's reputation for producing instruments of powerful tone, eminently suitable for a virtuoso violinist, was late in being appreciated and owed much to the genius of Niccolò Paganini.

WINE

A Collection of Domaine de la Romanée-Conti Methuselahs
Hong Kong HK$825,000
(£63,510; $106,589) 27.IV.98

An extraordinary collection of the seven wines from the Domaine de la Romanée-Conti, all in 6-litre Methuselah size and from the legendary 1985 vintage. Sold at Sotheby's inaugural Wine Auction in Hong Kong on 27th April 1998, these seven Methuselahs are amongst the best and most enduring Burgundies ever made – the millennium present from paradise.

Château Lafite 1959 CB
New York $12,937 (£7,891)
26.IX.97

The price achieved for this case of Château Lafite Rothschild 1959 attests to the rarity of finding top-quality wine in pristine condition packed in its original wooden case. The condition of the labels and capsules and the fill levels were all exceptional and undoubtedly contributed to the lot's success. It is a glorious wine and one of the greatest Lafites.

CARS AND AUTOMOBILIA

The Wakefield Trophy
Hallmarked *London 1935*,
stamped *Asprey London,
CJV Ltd*
Overall height 51 cm (20 in)
London £34,500 ($58,305)
24.XI.97

On 3 September 1935, Sir
Malcolm Campbell took
Bluebird out on to the
Bonneville Salt Flats to make
his attempt on the World
Land Speed record, which he
had set earlier that year at
276.82 miles per hour. After
two eventful runs through

the measured mile his
average speed was given as
301.129 mph and his ninth
and final World Land Speed
record was achieved. Sir
Humphrey Wakefield
presented Campbell with this
silver trophy engraved to
commemorate the event.

**1911 Rolls-Royce 40/50hp
D-fronted Landaulette**
London £496,500
($839,085) 24.XI.97

The Silver Ghost, described
as having '*ordre, luxe, calme,
volupté,* and *beauté* in a
degree not rivalled by any
other make or model',
maintained its supremacy
for 20 years. It is a matter
of history that Managing
Director Claude Johnson,
known as 'the hyphen in
Rolls-Royce', persuaded
Henry Royce to build the
Silver Ghost and concentrate
on its production, rather
than create a variety of
models each better than the
last. This example, chassis
number 1779, was delivered
to its owner, Major The
Hon Henry Guest, MP, in
March 1912; 85 years later
it completed the Scottish
Tour and won the coveted
'Best in Class' and 'Most
Elegant Car in Show'
awards at the Rolls-Royce
Enthusiasts Club
Annual Rally.

GARDEN STATUARY

A Bronze Fountain
Signed *G. Slot*, Danish, early
20th century
Height 197 cm (77½ in)
Sussex £74,100 ($120,042)
23.IX.97

This figure was cast at the
foundry Lauritz Rasumussen
in Copenhagen, which is
recorded as being active in
the early years of the 20th
century. Weathering has

produced a green patina on
the bronze, which effectively
unites the statue with its
surroundings.

**A Bronze Figure of a Young
Native American Hunter**
Ferdinand von Miller, signed
and dated *München 1873*
Height 1.85 m (6 ft 1 in)
New York $58,600 (£35,950)
25.VI.98
From the Collection of the
late Edward M. Pflueger and
Kathleen Powers Pflueger

Edward M. Pflueger, founder
and chairman of Baychem
Corporation, and his wife
were passionate collectors of
porcelain. The garden
statuary at their farm in
Dutchess County, New York
reflected this, with its
concentration on figures
with a classical or theatrical
theme. The sculptor of this
piece, Ferdinand von Miller,
also executed three
monumental sculptures of
Shakespeare, Columbus and
Homboldt, which are in the
St Louis Park in Missouri.

A Philippe Danfrie Gilt-brass Polyhedral Dial
French, last quarter
16th century
Height 25 cm (10 in)
London £309,500
($498,295) 30.IX.97

Philippe Danfrie was the leading maker of technical instruments in late 16th-century Paris, producing pieces of exceptional complexity and workmanship. Just over 20 instruments by Danfrie exist and this is the only known polyhedral dial. He was a versatile engraver whose activities ranged from the casting and cutting of printing-types, bookbinders' tools and dies for coins and medals to the invention, making and engraving of mathematical instruments and portrait sculpting in wax. Danfrie's career exemplifies the mixed milieu from which technical instrument-making developed in the 16th century. The quality and decoration of the instruments he made reflects the demands of his clients. In all his activities Danfrie served the court and seems himself to have been involved in the esoteric, humanist and mathematical culture that prevailed there.

A Long Sampler

English, c. 1660
Length 85 cm (33½ in),
width at widest point
24 cm (9½ in)
London £80,700 ($133,155)
5.III.98

Sadly this piece is not signed
or dated so the superb
needlewoman responsible
for it must remain
anonymous. It is surprising
that lace bands are not
incorporated in this sampler,
as was the custom. However,
it is probable that a
polychrome lace sampler
sold at Sotheby's in March
1997 for £62,000 was the
lace exercise for the piece
illustrated here, being the
test of embroidery
techniques and border
patterns by the same girl.

A Märklin Clockwork Paddle Steamer

c. 1900
Length 78.7 cm (31 in)
New York $108,100
(£64,860) 19.XII.97

The *Chicago* is in excellent
condition with only slight
repainting and repairing and,
although difficult to wind, the
paddle mechanism will turn.
The ship features a hand-
painted first-class deck with
draped windows and arched
entrance ways painted to give
the illusion of depth. It has
three plaster figures, one of
whom can be seen on the
three-tier captain's walk. The
boat remained in the same
family that purchased it at the
turn of the century, apparently
at the FAO Schwartz toyshop
in New York.

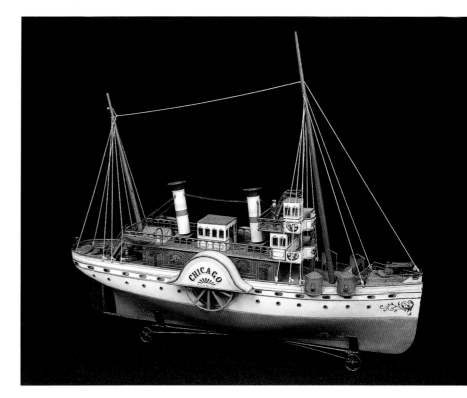

Original Hand-watercoloured and Inked Krazy Kat Specialty Piece
George Herriman, 1941,
King Features Syndicate
37.5 by 34.9 cm (14¾ by
13¾ in)
New York $11,500 (£7,015)
5.VI.98

The strength and charm of this design, sometimes lacking in other single panel colour works from the artist, belies its simplicity. The giant molar in the upper right-hand corner in place of the typical Arizona mesa and the perplexed look on the faces of all three characters gives this original a special place among the desert scenes that Herriman created from the 1920s to 1930s.

A Henry's Rifled Golf Ball
c. 1903
London £29,900 ($48,737)
10.VII.98

This type of ball was invented by Alexander Henry of Edinburgh and was rifled to precipitate straight trajectory in flight. This theory, however, did not work very well and few balls were produced. This was the first to have appeared at auction.

Thomas Hodge
'With a Putt Fair and Sure'
c. 1880, watercolour on card
14 by 10.5 cm (5½ by 4¼ in)
London £7,820 ($12,746)
10.VII.98

The red-coated golfer pictured here is H. S. C. Everard, historian and member of the Royal and Ancient Golf Club of St Andrews in Scotland, shown playing on the link.

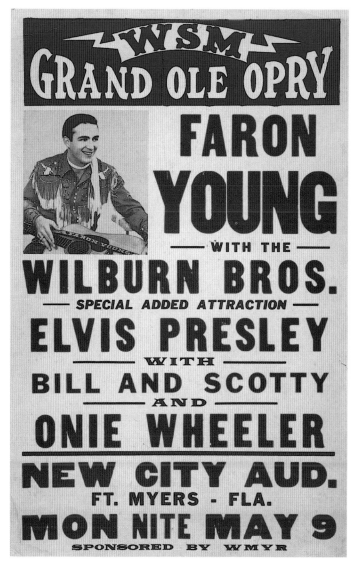

A *Men in Black* Poster
Columbia, 1934
104.1 by 68.6 cm (41 by 27 in)
New York $109,750
(£65,850) 4.IV.98

It was with *Men in Black* that the Three Stooges were recognized with an Academy Award nomination for best comedy short. This example is the earliest Columbia Three Stooges poster known to exist.

A Grand Ole Opry Elvis Presley Roadshow Poster
1955
New York $12,650 (£7,716)
13.VI.98

Uncle Brad's Hillbilly Hayride was presented by disc jockey Brad Lacey on WMYR, a radio station in Florida. The second show in a series of four sponsored by the station took place on 9th May 1955. Elvis Presley's first two performances that year were so well received that apparently Andy Griffith, the top-billed act for the third date, insisted that Presley himself close the show that night so as not to disappoint the (largely female) audience.

HOUSE SALES
The Roger Collection

In January, the darkest month of London's winter, Sotheby's was transformed by an event that was flamboyant, eclectic and colourful in character. Against the lilac walls of the salesrooms were displayed an extraordinary range of items, in a recreation of the interiors designed and lived in by the Roger brothers and made famous through articles in glossy magazines in the 1960s and 1970s. Over three days, from 28th to 30th January, the Chinese works of art collected by Alan, the Victorian furniture bought by Alistair ('Sandy') and the extravagantly elegant clothes worn by Neil ('Bunny') were sold to bidders eager to acquire a small part of the mystique that surrounded the three brothers.

Remarkable even to the most casual viewer was the way in which the sale highlighted the different aspects of the brothers' tastes, yet linking them all was the influence of their mother, Lady Roger, whose taste included Gothic furniture and a love of papier mâché, and who encouraged her sons to develop their interests. While Alan's love and understanding of the East translated into a collection of oriental works of art which also informed his approach to buying contemporary British art, and whereas Sandy – unusually for the time – collected Victorian paintings and Continental furniture, it was Bunny whose character dominated the collection, the press coverage and the public's attention.

Always exquisitely dressed, armed with bons mots and famous for his – sometimes notorious – parties, Bunny was a genuine 20th-century dandy. Included in the sale were his clothes, which numbered amongst them the mauve catsuit that he wore at the Amethyst Ball held to celebrate his 70th birthday in 1981, his dress kilts and the elegant, handmade suits that gave him his dapper look. The Victoria and Albert Museum Textile and Dress Collection actively acquired items from Bunny's wardrobe, including 32 shirts.

Witty, discerning and unexpected, this collection showed the Roger brothers to have had an understanding of the pleasure and diversity of life, to have wonderfully complemented each other, and to have had an 'eye' that never faltered.

ABOVE Lady Roger, wife of Sir Alexander Roger KCIE, and their three children (from left to right) Alan, Alastair ('Sandy') and Neil ('Bunny').

BELOW A view of the gallery with Bunny's Amethyst Ball catsuit.

Two Chinese Pots
Unmarked, probably early
18th century, height 32 cm
(12¾ in)
London £20,700 ($33,948)
29.1.98

**A Pair of William IV
Silver-gilt Casters**
John Bridge of Rundell,
Bridge & Rundell, London,
1829, height 21.5 cm (8½ in)
London £26,450 ($43,378)
29.1.98

**A Group of
Gentleman's Shirts**
Mainly 1960s and 1970s
London £2,070 ($3,395)
30.1.98

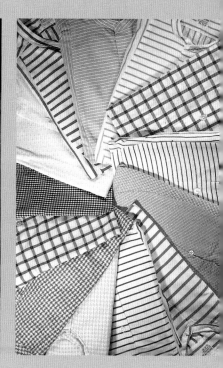

**A Carved Giltwood
Simulated Porphyry and
Marble-topped Console
Table**

19th century, in Egyptian
Revival Taste, 102 by 163 cm
(3 ft 4 in by 5 ft 4 in)
London £34,500 ($56,580)
28.1.98

**A 'Majolica' Umbrella and
Stick Stand**
T. C. Brown, Westhead
Moore & Co., c. 1880,
height 99 cm (39 in)

London £7,130 ($11,693)
28.1.98

**A Pair of Carved and
Stained Pine Hall Chairs**
19th century
London £5,175 ($8,487)
28.1.98

PRINCIPAL OFFICERS AND SPECIALISTS

Diana D. Brooks,
President and Chief Executive Officer

Richard E. Oldenburg,
Chairman, Sotheby's North & South America

John L. Marion,
Honorary Chairman, Sotheby's North & South America

William F. Ruprecht,
Managing Director, Sotheby's North & South America

John Block,
Vice Chairman, Sotheby's North & South America

Warren P. Weitman, Jr,
Vice Chairman, Sotheby's North & South America

Henry Wyndham,
Chairman, Sotheby's Europe

Princess de Beauvau Craon,
Deputy Chairman, Sotheby's Europe

David Bennett,
Deputy Chairman, Sotheby's Europe

Melanie Clore,
Deputy Chairman, Sotheby's Europe

The Hon James Stourton,
Deputy Chairman, Sotheby's Europe

James Miller,
Deputy Chairman, Sotheby's UK

George Bailey,
Co-Managing Director, Sotheby's Europe

Robin Woodhead,
Co-Managing Director, Sotheby's Europe

Simon Taylor,
Deputy Managing Director, Sotheby's Europe

Julian Thompson,
Co-Chairman, Sotheby's Asia

Alice Lam,
Co-Chairman, Sotheby's Asia

Please prefix all London telephone numbers with the code 0171, and all New York numbers with the code 212.

African & Oceanic Art
Jean G. Fritts
New York, 774 5360
London, 293 5116

American Decorative Arts & Furniture
Leslie B. Keno
New York, 606 7130
William W. Stahl, Jr
606 7110
Wendell Garrett
606 7137

American Folk Art
Nancy Druckman
New York, 606 7225

American Indian Art
Ellen Napiura Taubman
New York, 774 5370

American Paintings, Drawings & Sculpture
Peter Rathbone &
Dara Mitchell
New York, 606 7280

Antiquities
Richard M. Keresey &
R. Seth Bright
New York, 774 5390
London, 293 5109

Arms, Armour & Medals
Nicholas McCullough
Sussex, 01403 833540
Margaret Schwartz
New York, 606 7260

Books & Manuscripts
Dr Stephen Roe
London, 293 5286
David N. Redden
New York, 774 5322

British Pictures
David Moore-Gwyn
(*1500 to 1850*) London,
293 5406
James Miller (*1500 to 1850*)
293 5405
Henry Wemyss
(*Watercolours*)
293 5409
Martin Gallon (*Victorian*)
293 5386
Simon Taylor (*Victorian*)
293 5385
Susannah Pollen
(*20th Century*)
293 5388

Ceramics
Peter Arney
London, 293 5134
Letitia Roberts
New York, 774 5325

Chinese Art
James B. Godfrey
New York, 606 7332
Julian Thompson
London, 293 5371
Henry Howard-Sneyd &
Colin Mackay 293 5147/5
Noah Kupferman (*Paintings*)
New York, 606 7334

Clocks & Watches
Michael Turner (*Clocks*)
London, 293 5329
Tina Millar (*Watches*)
293 5328
Daryn Schnipper
New York, 744 5313

Coins and Medals
Tom Eden (*Ancient & Islamic*)
London, 293 5313
James Morton (*English & Paper Money*)
293 5314
Edward Playfair (*Medals*)
293 5709
Paul Song
New York, 606 7856

Collectibles
Dana Hawkes
New York, 606 7910
Jon Baddeley
London, 293 5205

Contemporary Art
Tobias Meyer
New York, 606 7254
Leslie Prouty
606 7254
Elena Geuna
London, 293 5401
Florence de Botton
Paris, 33 (1) 53 05 53 05

English Furniture & Decorations
Joseph Friedman
London, 293 5474
Graham Child
293 5347
Larry J. Sirolli
New York, 606 7577
William W. Stahl, Jr
606 7110

European Works of Art
Elizabeth Wilson
London, 293 5321
Margaret Schwartz
New York, 606 7250

Fashion
Tiffany Dubin
New York, 774 5304

French & Continental Furniture & Decorations
Mario Tavella
London, 293 5052
Phillips Hathaway
New York, 606 7213
Thierry Millerand
606 7213
Alexandre Pradère
Paris, 33 (1) 53 05 53 05

Garden Statuary & Architectural Items
James Rylands
Sussex, 01403 833559
Elaine Whitmire
New York, 606 7285

Glass & Paperweights
Lauren K. Tarshis
New York, 774 5325
Simon Cottle
London, 293 5133

**Impressionist &
Modern Art**
Alexander Apsis
New York, 606 7360
John L. Tancock
606 7360
Melanie Clore
London, 293 5394
Philip Hook
293 5223
Michel Strauss
293 5389
Andrew Strauss
Paris, 33 (1) 53 05 53 05

**Indian & Southeast
Asian Art**
Carlton C. Rochell, Jr
New York, 606 7304
Marcus Fraser
London, 293 5332

Islamic Art & Carpets
Marcus Fraser (*Works of Art*)
London, 293 5332
Jacqueline Coulter (*Carpets*)
293 5152
Richard M. Keresey
(*Works of Art*)
New York, 774 5360
Mary Jo Otsea (*Carpets*)
606 7996

Japanese Art
Neil Davey &
Max Rutherston
London, 293 5141
Ryoichi Iida &
Gretchen Good
New York, 606 7338

Jewellery
John D. Block
New York, 606 7392
David Bennett
Geneva, 41 (22) 908 4841
Alexandra Rhodes
London, 293 5311
Lisa Hubbard
Hong Kong, 2523 5438

Judaica
David Breuer-Weil
Tel Aviv, 972 (3) 560 1666
Camilla Previté
London, 293 5334
David Redden (*Books*)
New York, 606 7386
Kevin Tierney (*Silver*)
606 7160

Korean Works of Art
Henry Howard-Sneyd
London, 293 5147
Ryoichi Iida & Jiyoung Koo
New York, 606 7286

Latin American Art
Isabella Hutchinson
New York, 606 7290

Musical Instruments
Graham Wells
London, 293 5341
Rachel Gaul
New York, 606 7938

**19th Century European
Furniture & Works of Art**
Jonathan Meyer
London, 293 5350
Elaine Whitmire
New York, 606 7285

**19th Century European
Paintings & Drawings**
Michael Bing
London, 293 5380
Nancy Harrison & Benjamin
Doller
New York, 606 7140
Pascale Pavageau
Paris, 33 (1) 53 05 53 05
Eveline van Oirschot
Amsterdam 31 (20) 550 2200

**19th & Early 20th Century
Sculpture**
Diana Keith Neal
London, 293 5337
Christopher Gow
New York, 606 7145

**Old Master Paintings &
Drawings**
Alexander Bell
London, 293 5420
Gregory Rubinstein
(*Drawings*)
293 5417
George Wachter
New York, 606 7230
Scott Schaefer (*Drawings*)
606 7230
Frédéric Gourd
Paris, 33 (1) 53 05 53 05
Julien Stock
Rome, 39 (6) 69 94 17 91

Oriental Manuscripts
Marcus Fraser
London, 293 5332
Carlton C. Rochell, Jr
New York, 606 7304

Photographs
Philippe Garner
London, 293 5138
Denise Bethel
New York, 606 7240

Portrait Miniatures & Vertu
Gerard Hill
New York, 606 7150
Haydn Williams
London, 293 5326
Heinrich Graf von Spreti
Munich, 49 (89) 291 31 51

Postage Stamps
Richard Ashton
London, 293 5224
Robert A.G.A. Scott
New York, 606 7915

Pre-Columbian Art
Stacy Goodman
New York, 774 5360
Fatma Turkkan-Wille
Zurich, 41 (1) 202 3003

Prints
Nancy Bialler (*Old Master*)
Mary Bartow (*19th & 20th
Century*)
New York, 606 7117
Nina del Rio (*Contemporary*)
606 7113
Jonathan Pratt
London, 293 5212

Russian Paintings & Icons
Alice Milica Ilich
London, 293 5325
Gerard Hill
New York, 606 7150

Silver
Kevin Tierney & Ian Irving
New York, 606 7160
Peter Waldron (*English*)
London, 293 5104
Harold Charteris
(*Continental*)
293 5106
Kobus du Plessis
Paris, 33 (1) 53 05 53 05

Sporting Guns
Adrian Weller
Sussex, 01403 833575

20th Century Applied Arts
Barbara E. Deisroth
New York, 606 7170
Philippe Garner
London, 293 5138

Vintage Cars
Peter Blond
London, 293 5320
Richard Crump
New York, 606 7920

Western Manuscripts
Dr Christopher de Hamel,
FSA
London, 293 5330

Wine
Serena Sutcliffe, MW
London, 293 5045
Jamie Ritchie
New York, 774 5330

Sotheby's Institute
Kathleen Martin
New York, 606 7822
Anne Ceresole
London, 462 3232

Tax & Heritage
James Jowitt
London, 293 5335

Trusts & Estates
Lindsey Pryor
New York, 848 2622

Valuations
Hon James Stourton
London, 293 5435
Lindsey Pryor
New York, 848 2622
Diederik Westerhuis
Amsterdam,
31 (20) 550 2200

**Sotheby's Financial
Services**
Shelley Fischer
New York, 508 8061
Catherine Chiarella
508 8067
Ann-Marie Casey-Jones
London, 293 5028

**Sotheby's International
Realty**
Stuart N. Siegel, President,
New York, 606 4100

Business Development
Warren P. Weitman, Jr
New York, 606 7198

**Sotheby's World Wide
Web Site**
http://www.sothebys.com

INDEX

Acknowledgements
Prices given throughout include the buyer's premium applicable in the saleroom concerned. These prices are shown in the currency in which they were realized. The sterling and dollar equivalent figures, shown in brackets, are based upon the rates of exchange on the day of the sale.

The editor would like to thank Luke Rittner, William F. Ruprecht, Paul Donaher, Ken Adlard, Rachel Hagan, Margaret Pugliese, Daisy Edelson, Lesley Bartlett, Jennifer Conner, Lucinda Blythe, Tara Heffler, Diane Pia, Tim Robson and all the Sotheby's departments for their help with this book.

Photographic Acknowledgements
The editor would like to thank the following photographers and organizations for their kind permission to reproduce the photographs in *Art At Auction 1997–1998* (r – right, l – left, t – top, b – below):
© ADAGP, Paris and DACS London 1998, pp. 78, 79, 85, 87, 88, 93, 95
© Ken Adlard/Sotheby's, endpapers, pp. 8 (l), 10 (t), 18 (b), 20 (l), 24 (t), 28 (tl), 29 (br), 34 (t & r), 35, 40
© David Hays/Sotheby's, pp. 12 (b), 22 (tr), 30 (t), 34 (tl), 36 (t), 38 (t), 42 (b)
© Itamar Grinberg/Sotheby's, p. 10 (b)
© Leslie Jean-Bart/Sotheby's, pp. 27 (b), 33 (b)
© Betty Marshall/Sotheby's, p. 7
© ARS, New York and DACS, London 1998, p. 74, 92
© DACS 1998, p. 17 (t), 69, 86, 98 (tr)
© Kate Rothko Prizel & Christopher Rothko/DACS 1998, p. 91
© The Andy Warhol Foundation/ARS, New York and DACS London 1998, front cover, pp. 26, 100 (bl)
© Succession Picasso/DACS 1998, p. 89
© Estate of Morris Hirschfield/VAGA, New York/ DACS, London 1998, p. 147 (b)
© Estate of Stuart Davies/VAGA, New York/DACS, London 1998, p. 75
© Estate of Sir John Lavery, 1998, p. 63
© Anne & Michael Yeats 1998, p. 9
© Walter Richard Sickert/DACS 1998, p. 64
© Claes Oldenburg 1998, p. 100
© Gerhard Richter 1998, p. 97

Every effort has been made to trace the copyright of the images used in this book. Sotheby's apologises for any errors or omissions.